THE
MIND AT
LARGE

THE MIND AT LARGE

CLAIRVOYANCE, PSYCHICS, POLICE AND LIFE AFTER DEATH: A POLISH PERSPECTIVE

ZOFIA WEAVER & KRZYSZTOF JANOSZKA

www.whitecrowbooks.com

Published by White Crow Books; an imprint of White Crow Productions Ltd.

For information, contact White Crow Books by e-mail: info@whitecrowbooks.com.

Cover Design by Astrid@Astridpaints.com
Interior design by Velin@Perseus-Design.com

Paperback: ISBN: 978-1-78677-212-1
eBook: ISBN: 978-1-78677-213-8

Fiction / BODY, MIND & SPIRIT / Parapsychology /
ESP, Clairvoyance, Precognition, Telepathy.

www.whitecrowbooks.com

In memory of Marek Rymuszko whose
friendship, support and inspiration
made this book possible

PRAISE FOR *THE MIND AT LARGE*

Before entering the field of parapsychology, I earned a Master of Criminology degree. My dual interests are not unique. Even Cesare Lombroso – one of the founders of scientific criminology – was also a contributor to the field of psychical research. There is a complex history of psychics working with law enforcement agencies. I know from personal experience that this history is punctuated with numerous uncanny successes that, realistically, can only be attributed to various forms of clairvoyance and precognition. This book, *The Mind At Large* written by Zofia Weaver and Krzysztof Janoszka, constitutes a major contribution to the literature in this area. It merits serious study, particularly by those associated with law enforcement and criminology.

~ **Jeffrey Mishlove, PhD,**
Host and Producer of New Thinking Allowed

Brilliant! This is the best book on clairvoyance I've read in years. Zofia Weaver and Krzysztof Janoszka covered all important historical and theoretical aspects of this fascinating phenomenon in a masterfully lucid way. In addition, they brought barely known gems from practice to the attention of a Western audience: Backed up with reprints of original police reports, they described the work of contemporary Polish clairvoyant Krzysztof Jackowski who helped to solve dozens of criminal acts in cooperation with the Polish police. His documented clairvoyant impressions clearly rank among the most impressive psi experiences on record. The authors also tackle the question of the source of these clairvoyant visions. Is it "ordinary" clairvoyance or are the deceased also involved, such as murdered victims? Read the book and form your own opinion... you won't regret it.

~ **Michael Nahm, PhD,** Institute for Frontier Areas of
Psychology and Mental Health, Freiburg, Germany

Who – what – are we? The question is perennial. Something small in power, trapped by time, locked in mortal bodies? Others – philosophers, poets, mystics, even scientists – hold that we are inlets to a greater reality, part of a higher life and fuller mode of being.

The Mind at Large is a book that argues that the dimensions of our personality far outstrip our ordinary selves. The authors do so by laying out many strands of extraordinary, documented data, all of which point to powers of the mind that extend our human nature and point to its transcendent potential.

A special feature focuses on Polish police records for examples of the dramatic use of clairvoyance solving crimes and mysteries in the thick of real life. This book will expand your sense of identity, by providing solid clues to how we connect to the greater mind at large.

~ **Michael Grosso, PhD,**
author of *Smile of the Universe: Miracles in an Age of Disbelief*

"Parapsychological naturalist" has been used to describe the lead author's approach to anomalous phenomena. This whole book provides a strong case for why experiences in the natural world (spontaneous phenomena), and studying in meticulous details those who claim anomalous abilities, hold a vital place within parapsychological research. Many may think that the parapsychologist now only spends their time in the laboratory, quantifying studies of psychic ability. On the contrary, all approaches complement the bigger picture and the difficult questions.

The natural world and observations of exceptional phenomena can tell us many things, especially, what conventional mechanisms are at work, how to dig deeper when none present themselves, what questions we should be asking, and how anything may transfer to the laboratory – if at all possible? The latter is not always achievable or ecologically valid. The natural world is beautifully time consuming, but worth the wait for the discoveries we can make. The authors should be commended for going forth into the field and their detailed presentations of the literature and cases."

~ **Dr Callum E. Cooper,**
Psychologist, Author and Science Promotor

ACKNOWLEDGMENTS

~

A great debt of gratitude is due to Krzysztof Jackowski, the clairvoyant whose contribution to our understanding of clairvoyance is one of the main themes of this book. Warmest thanks are also due to Julie Billingham and David Rousseau for their most constructive comments on the earlier draft, and to our publisher, Jon Beecher, for his unwavering support and helpful advice.

CONTENTS

~

FOREWORD

~

I t gives me great pleasure to introduce this work and the person who brought it to fruition, Dr Zofia Weaver. In my view this material represents the best evidence ever obtained for the human ability to make observations beyond the range of our physical senses, an ability commonly called clairvoyance (literally meaning 'clear sight') but also known under other terms such as 'remote viewing'. Moreover, the presentation of this evidence is led by the person who is arguably the best qualified to assess and convey it.

Although this volume formally has two authors, it is really the achievement of three people. First, the Polish clairvoyant Krzysztof Jackowski, who for the past two decades has used his talent to support detective work by the Polish police. Uniquely, he insisted on receiving written confirmation of the value of his help at every step, thus building up a substantial archive of objective assessments of the practical value of his work and his talent. Second, the Polish detective Krzysztof Janoszka, who studied these cases academically and successfully advocated, despite much initial resistance, that the police should publicly acknowledge Jackowski for the extraordinary help they received. And third, but by no means least, Zofia Weaver, who realised both the importance this data has for the academic study of psychical abilities and the urgency of bringing it to the attention of psychical researchers worldwide.

Zofia was born and initially educated in Poland. She built on her Polish Baccalaureate with a BA (Hons) in Slavonic Studies and a PhD in Slavonic Linguistics from the University of Nottingham, UK. She divides her time between Poland and the UK, and has worked for more than 20 years translating into English various Polish works in areas as diverse as commerce, science and music. In a particular area of focus, she has translated musicological texts for the Polish Academy of Sciences, the University of Warsaw, Jagiellonian University, the "Warsaw Autumn" festival of contemporary music and others, including significant large-scale translation projects.

I have known Zofia for more than twenty years as a fellow member of the governing Council of the Society for Psychical Research (SPR). The SPR, founded in London in 1882, was the first organization established to investigate, in a scientific spirit, phenomena which are *prima facie* inexplicable on any generally recognised hypothesis. This quest continues today, as amply demonstrated by the SPR's conferences, magazine, Journal, Proceedings, online Psi Encyclopedia and extensive libraries and archives. Zofia was invited to the role of Editor of the Society's Journal and served in this capacity from 1999 to 2002, continuing as Associate Editor in the present day.

Her own studies in psychical research have focused largely on Polish mediums, most importantly the extraordinary physical medium Franek Kluski and the clairvoyant Stefan Ossowiecki. Some of the greatest clairvoyants of all time were Polish, and Zofia, as a native Polish speaker, could access many original sources unknown and impenetrable to English researchers. She is determined to ensure that the historical research done with great Polish mediums and published in Polish and French is made accessible to researchers in the English-speaking world. This has resulted in the production of three books prior to the present volume, and several journal articles.

These works include her recently completed (2022) translation of Okołowicz's 1926 book *Reminiscences of Séances with the Medium Franek Kluski,* with additional research and commentary by her and her co-researcher Michael Nahm, her 2015 book *Other Realities: The Enigma of Franek Kluski's Mediumship,* and her 2005 book *A World in a Grain of Sand: The Clairvoyance of Stefan Ossowiecki.* Details of these and other works by Zofia can be found in the entry about her in the SPR's online *Psi Encyclopedia.* The last-mentioned book was co-authored with Ian Stevenson (well known for his university-based research on cases suggestive of reincarnation), and Mary Rose Barrington, a Vice President of the SPR and long term researcher in physical mediumship, poltergeists and the so-called 'disappearing object phenomenon', on which she published an important book in 2018.

In fact, I first learned of Zofia through Mary Rose Barrington, a mutual friend, even before meeting her personally. Zofia had joined the

SPR in the early 1980s and was drawn to Mary Rose by their common interest in clairvoyants, particularly the exceptional Polish ones. Zofia's enthusiasm in this area, and Mary Rose's support for it, energised the effort to produce the works mentioned above.

Over the years, Zofia and I have both been involved in a number of projects, including the 2010 redevelopment of the SPR website and a project initiated by the Centre for Fundamental and Anomalies Research (C-FAR) aimed at building a database of paradigm-challenging cases. Through these projects I have come to admire and respect her deep knowledge of the data from psychical research, her open-minded approach, her pragmatic wisdom about the inevitable tensions in this controversial field, and her irrepressible enthusiasm and optimism in engaging with the strange and controversial phenomena that characterise the field of psychical research generally and physical mediumship in particular.

Zofia particularly values 'ecologically authentic' psychical research, a mode of research very different from laboratory-based 'experimental' research. The former kind explores psychical phenomena in their natural habitat, so to speak. It is more likely to produce dramatic results, but the exceptional persons producing such phenomena are quite rare and psychologically diverse, and the research conditions are much more challenging to control. Consequently, the results may be more striking but also more difficult to interpret in a confident and unambiguous way. That said, the outcomes might be more impressive and more diverse than those that experimental research can deliver, and hence the implications for theoretical insights might be more profound. Therefore, ecologically authentic research may offer us a more direct route to understanding the actual limitations and biases of the current scientific paradigm, while simultaneously opening up opportunities for research towards a paradigm that better represents the way things (and we) actually are, and more clearly reveals what the limits of our true potential might actually be. A prime example of such ecologically authentic research is that involving especially talented clairvoyants engaging with real-world problems and questions.

Zofia is a 'parapsychological naturalist', a term introduced by philosopher Stephan Braude, meaning that she regards making careful observations more highly than upholding or building theories, and is highly sensitive to the presence of suppositions that can bias the making of observations and the building of theories. Prizing data over theory and prizing open-mindedness over orthodoxy represents a rare but invaluable attitude when investigating anomalous or extraordinary human experiences.

Her talents, experience and attitude combine to make her uniquely well-qualified to have led the project that produced the current book. Once again there is a great Polish medium involved, but this time it is a person still living and working as a medium, and we have a large body of contemporary records made by qualified and credible witnesses. And the cases are often breathtakingly surprising. One could hardly ask for better-documented and more interesting case records than are presented here. The subject matter is well-served to have found a voice for this material in Zofia Weaver, who not only helps to make the case material vivid but also gently guides the reader through the conceptual landscape in which these cases strive to be accommodated. This she does not to present conclusions to be drawn but to encourage more and wider exploration in this and other relevant fields. Her erudition and level-headed treatment make for an engaging and compelling book that will, no doubt, soon become a modern classic in mediumship studies. In my view, its publication marks a most important and seminal moment in clairvoyance research. I highly recommend it, and I foresee that it will inspire a wide readership to explore further the possibility that our actual senses can reach beyond the limits of our known physical ones, and to reflect on what this possibility might mean for our understanding of what we are and how we relate to each other and to the world. That, I believe, is the true value of this work.

David Rousseau PhD BEng FRSA
2022

1

AN EXTRAORDINARY
CLAIRVOYANT AND AN
EXTRAORDINARY POLICEMAN

~

Why and how this book came about

Clairvoyance does not fit into the mainstream scientific worldview of the Western world. Becoming aware of objects or events that are beyond the reach of physical senses is simply not possible in the world of space and time according to the current scientific model. Science concerns itself with natural phenomena so stories of "supernatural powers" belong with belief systems, not evidence-based models of patterns observed in nature. Such stories are dismissed as anecdotes, products of human imagination and desire for meaning, combined with failures of memory and observation.

However, accounts of anomalous phenomena occur throughout human history and on closer examination form regular patterns. There are a number of organisations that collect and study such reports; the oldest of them is the Society for Psychical Research (SPR) formed in the UK in 1882. By now there exists a large amount of data, based both on spontaneous reports and experiments, that testifies to its existence regardless of how it is interpreted.

I have been researching such data for some decades now. Being Polish by birth, I focus my research on Polish contributions to the subject, and bringing them to the English-speaking audience.

It is more than twenty years since I first heard of the Polish clairvoyant Krzysztof Jackowski. At that time I had already been a member of the SPR for many years, and was then editor of the Society's *Journal*. My personal interests focused on research into mediumship in Poland, which, prior to the Second World War, had a fascinating history of experimentation and some exceptional mediums (Barrington et al., 2005; Weaver, 2015). I was already working on a volume about the famous Polish clairvoyant Stefan Ossowiecki, so hearing about someone who seemed equally gifted but was actually living was very exciting.

Jackowski's name became more prominent because of a case in the mid-1990s. The case in question took place in 1994-95 and involved three men who disappeared while on a business trip to Kaliningrad (Koenigsberg). Their families asked Jackowski for help and using a photograph of one of the men he sensed that the man was dead, as were his companions; their throats had been cut and they had been decapitated. The clairvoyant could hardly believe what he saw but when he tried again he saw three headless bodies in a forest at a specific location. Understandably, the families did not want to believe it but a few days later Russian police revealed that the bodies had been found as Jackowski had described. The killer turned out to be a business contact of the three men, who, by cutting off their heads, tried to divert suspicion to the local mafia who executed informers in this way. Jackowski did not contribute to the finding of the bodies on that occasion, but the story got into the media, who were impressed by the accurate description of the bodies and their position. The case catapulted him into the public eye.

The first book about Jackowski and his gift, *Jasnowidz z Człuchowa. Moje tajemnice* [*The Clairvoyant from Człuchów. My secrets*], appeared in 2000 (Szczesiak, 2000). It described more than 40 cases from the period 1994-1999, many of them confirmed in writing, some officially by the police forces in question, and included interviews with the police officers and families involved. There were cases of locating bodies of missing persons who had drowned – a murder case confirmed by the police officer in charge – all of them with precise descriptions of people and places (in one case, of exactly how a man committed suicide, including the kind of string used).

I contacted the author of the book, who assured me that the documentation did exist, and its contents were confirmed by other reliable sources. In 2001 I contacted Jackowski himself, and he was very keen to cooperate in any experiments that the SPR might propose, with the caveat that, unlike his hero Stefan Ossowiecki, he was unable to "read" through envelopes.

And then life took a different course and our plans came to nothing. My personal situation changed suddenly because of serious illness in my family, and the experiments never took place. But now I think that no amount of experimenting would have tested Jackowski's range of clairvoyance in the way that the real-life cases tested it during the years that followed. Throughout those years he insisted on written official confirmations of his contributions to solving criminal cases from the various police forces and he kept letters from institutions and private persons acknowledging his help.

By this time, his vastly expanded documentation has also been examined in depth and verified by the co-author of this book, Krzysztof Janoszka (pronounced Yanoshka), who, when Jackowski's story began, was just a child. This has created a dossier of case studies that is a significant addition to the evidence for and understanding of clairvoyance, particularly in the area of psychic detection, where reliable records are few. It also means that since the start of his [Jackowski's] career there have been twenty more years of research into clairvoyance and its connection to mediumship.

On a wider scale, there have been significant developments in the study of consciousness and related areas, and they may point to ways of accommodating this dossier and its implications within a scientific context.

Police Sergeant Krzysztof Janoszka

In November 2014, Krzysztof Janoszka, then a student at the Police Academy in Poland, contacted the SPR. He had written a diploma thesis on the use of psychics in police work and wanted to draw our attention to the phenomena demonstrated by Jackowski. By now (2022), as well as having become a qualified police officer (CID sergeant at the City Police Headquarters in his home city), he has also written a book based on his thesis and on interviews with Jackowski (Janoszka, 2018). Thanks to Janoszka there is now in the public domain plenty of valid documentation supporting specific cases.

Janoszka graduated from the Police Academy in Szczytno in 2014. Becoming a student at the Police Academy (the only higher education establishment of this kind in Poland) was for him a dream come true. He was happy there, meeting many wonderful people and acquiring essential skills and knowledge.

He became particularly interested in the problem of people trafficking and studied the subject, which resulted in The Academy's awarding him a prize for the best licentiate thesis for his work on children as victims of trafficking. He specialised in criminology and internal security and is a graduate of Gdańsk University with a Master's degree in criminology; he also has a Master's degree from Warsaw University's Faculty of Law and Administration.

Krzysztof has been working as a police officer since 2015, starting out as a "front line" constable; he is now a sergeant and sees his future in the police force. He therefore comes to the subject of parapsychology from a different perspective, and with a different set of experiences (such as "having eyes in the back of your head" while on patrol) from those who write about clairvoyance and detection (not that there is much written on it), who tend to be parapsychologists or journalists.

His research, written up as a dissertation for his Master's degree at Warsaw University, provides much of the material in this book, particularly in Chapters 6 and 7. Its title is *The use of parapsychology in investigative work on the example of the cooperation between Polish police and the clairvoyant Krzysztof Jackowski* (Janoszka, 2014).

Janoszka learnt about Jackowski from the media and from contacts with police officers while still a student at the Police Academy, and encountered an ethical and philosophical problem. He could not reconcile what he learnt about the actual criminal and missing person cases that involved the clairvoyant and had been confirmed by the police officers, who worked with him, with the denial of what looked like obvious facts by the official police spokespersons. So he decided to investigate these cases for himself. One step he took in the investigation was to invite Jackowski to give a lecture to the independent students' association at the Police Academy.

Janoszka visited the clairvoyant at home in December 2012 to present the invitation and was both surprised by the modest circumstances in which he lived and fascinated by what he had to say.

The very idea of discussing such a subject turned out to be unacceptable to the higher authorities, who were fearful of damaging the image of the police, and the students were ordered to call off the talk after it had been announced in the local press. The move backfired resulting in media accusations of double standards and suppression of freedom of speech. The students protested and even the President of the Police Generals' Association intervened on their behalf to no avail. However, despite the controversy, the lecture finally took place a year later in December 2013 away from the Academy's premises.

Janoszka's interest in clairvoyance and its use by the police caused him quite a lot of trouble on a personal level, at the start of his intended career in the police force. In the end he got away with only being given a warning for infringing the Academy's internal regulations, a minor misdemeanour. One of the lecturers told him that nobody expected a rank-and-file student to risk his future career by putting forward an opinion different from the official policy of the Headquarters.

But that episode made him decide to take a closer look at how the police collaborated with Jackowski and he examined that relationship in his diploma thesis. His aim was to document a number of criminal cases where the police used Jackowski by interviewing the police officers involved and other experts in law and criminology. Alongside this project his acquaintance with Jackowski turned into friendship and resulted in a book of Janoszka's interviews with the clairvoyant (Janoszka, 2018). Much of the verified evidence presented here and supported by interviews with those involved stems from that book, alongside the material from the already mentioned Master's thesis (Janoszka, 2014).

The book brought Janoszka media attention and an invitation to lecture at the Polish Forensics Association.

He started out with an endearing and idealistic inability to understand the degree to which people, particularly in positions of power, can be driven by their beliefs and prejudices rather than evidence. In his book he gives examples of this, such as a situation where the attitude "we don't believe in such things" drives sceptics to leave discussions before being forced to examine verified accounts – an attitude also not unknown among academic circles in the West. Clinging to ignorance is safer, and denial of anything smacking of the "esoteric" is the norm in a world where mainstream science adopts materialism (or physicalism) as the only acceptable philosophy.

In an interview with Janoszka, a journalist, Robert Bernatowicz, noted that it would be an act of great courage for some people in positions of authority, in the academia or elsewhere, to admit to being open to examining such issues (Janoszka, 2014, p. 104).

"Telepathy does not exist," claimed one of the most popular Polish dailies. "No clairvoyant has ever contributed to finding a missing person," said the press office of the Police Headquarters. "Contacting a clairvoyant can be a painful experience for the families of missing persons, and we don't know of any cases where this helped," claims ITAKA, the Centre for Locating Missing Persons. "Clairvoyance is a way of contacting demons," says the Roman Catholic Church.

In such a climate, with the press often manipulating the facts, it is hardly surprising that the police give out contradictory statements. One of the main dailies published an attack on Jackowski at the very time when the police magazine (published under the aegis of the Police Headquarters) presented information based on police documentation that confirmed the accounts published on Jackowski's own webpage. These reports stated that the clairvoyant contributed to solving dozens of cases by providing detailed, accurate information unknown to him by normal means. As Janoszka pointed out, the claim by the official police spokesperson that these were vague formulaic acknowledgments issued out of politeness would mean that dozens of police officers were committing offences by telling lies.

It needs to be stressed that the official attitude of the Polish police is not unique; using psychics continues to be an embarrassing subject for police forces in other countries. This is hardly surprising since clairvoyance is not a recognised human ability; it's surrounded by controversy and provides good feeding ground for the media, with many extraordinary claims and counter claims (see chapter 6). It also needs to be borne in mind that Jackowski's clairvoyance is not a unique gift; there is much reliable evidence, both experimental and anecdotal, that testifies to the reality of the phenomenon (chapters 4 and 5). What makes his case unique is the fact that for years now, he has insisted on having his contributions to specific police cases confirmed in writing at the time. There is also a multitude of letters from private persons acknowledging his help. We should bear in mind that in the case of missing persons, everyone involved in the search is blind to the location of the target, while Jackowski is blind to any information about the case except maybe a photo or personal possession. This is solid empirical evidence in real life cases. His dossier is a unique set of evidence for clairvoyance outside the lab.

In many thoroughly verified cases, Jackowski has provided details of which he could not possibly be aware of by normal means. These abilities could be tested in laboratory conditions (and in fact the clairvoyant has successfully taken part in a number of tests and competitions, also outside Poland), but such tests provide limited information and little insight into clairvoyance when compared to real-life cases. Experiments such as, for example, identifying an object in a box, are a far cry from a linked continuum of specific details that match a particular real situation and lead to, for example, locating a specific body. Such clairvoyant "visions", or "readings" are spontaneous, irregular and not repeatable to order, but they do exist. It is impossible to offer a reliable assessment of Jackowski's rate of success, as many of his cases are undocumented. On the basis of the reasonably well documented accounts Janoszka estimates Jackowski's accuracy rate to be about 50-60%, which is close to the estimates of success in remote viewing[1] (with 65% reliability being "tops") offered by Joe McMoneagle, one of the most well-regarded remote viewers in the West today (McMoneagle, 2000, pp. 27-33).

Janoszka hoped his book would make a contribution to a better understanding of parapsychology as a subject. The issue also involved principles of standing up for what is just and fair. In Janoszka's own words:

"I could not accept that an institution that relied so much on Jackowski's help was also denying it, and that in spite of the evidence he was being treated as a cheat and a charlatan. My only motivation was to tell the truth." (Janoszka, 2018, p. 248)

Finally, owing to Janoszka's efforts, in May 2016 the National Police Headquarters in Poland officially acknowledged Jackowski's positive contribution to police investigations and, in recognition of his extraordinary skills, issued a statement expressing gratitude "for [his] collaboration and help on numerous occasions in searching for missing persons and investigations of unexplained crimes." It was signed by the Commissioners and Leaders of Regional Criminal Investigations Departments.

So who is this clairvoyant whose activities cause such controversy?

Krzysztof Jackowski.

Krzysztof Jackowski does not fit the conventional image of a psychic. There were no special experiences in his childhood, no encounters with apparitions, no visions of dead relatives and no precognitive dreams.

---

[1]   Remote viewing involves a special protocol but it is a form of clairvoyance.

He was born in 1963 into a very ordinary family. They came from a poor village and moved to the small town of Człuchów [in Pomerania, in northwestern Poland] in the early 1960s in search of work. He has two brothers and two sisters, and his parents worked hard as cleaner and orderly in the local school and hospital to support the family. They lived in an old dilapidated block of flats but there were gardens and a lake at the back. Being somewhat of a loner he would spend a lot of time there. Człuchów is a county capital, an attractive place with easy links to the rest of Poland, and is still Jackowski's home. However, in the 1960s, without the access to knowledge that we now take for granted thanks to the Internet, and without family support for his intellectual curiosity, it was a bleak life for a bright and curious youngster.

As a teenager he was very interested in astronomy and science, but, since books about such subjects were not easily accessible, he would look for discarded books on science at the local wastepaper collection point. At the age of fifteen he had two articles published in a youth science magazine. Albert Einstein was his hero and young Jackowski had his picture on the wall, but his mother burnt it to make sure he attended to schoolwork. It is, therefore, not surprising that he prayed to be someone else, rebelling against the greyness of his life. While there was no obvious childhood trauma, which is common in people with psychic abilities, when you read his autobiography you cannot help but feel that he was much too bright for his environment, and that must have been a source of constant frustration.

He trained and worked as a machine operator, still reading science books even at work (setting up the machinery so that it needed minimum supervision). He married when he was 21, worked all hours to support his family, and experienced a period of depression and self-examination (Szczesiak, 2000, p. 194).

He did not start having strange experiences until his late twenties, although as a child he did frequently dream of the dead and now suspects that this was somehow part of what he has come to regard as his ability to link to the dead. The only strange thing was the occasional feeling of "pins and needles" or pressure in his forehead, associated with some danger or obstacle. At the time he thought everyone was like that. He now associates this feeling with his later clairvoyant experiences, with the forehead somehow involved as a kind of sensor, as if the energy from an object or photograph that he holds close enters through his forehead. He would also obsessively arrange sharp objects, such as knives and forks, so that they would face in one direction and away from him, and would often stroke the corners of objects, as if they were itching and needed scratching.

His early experiences were simple precognitions of things about to happen. Once he was "forced" to go up to an elderly man in the street and warn him that he had acute appendicitis and should immediately go to hospital – and the man said he was on the way there (something that would also sometimes happen to another Polish medium Stefan Ossowiecki, who is examined in a later chapter).

Jackowski approached the health & safety inspector at work having heard he was interested in anomalous phenomena and the inspector took his account about the elderly man seriously, testing him by showing him photographs of strangers and asking him to comment on them.

He started reading books on parapsychology and formed an astronomy and parapsychology interest group at the local community centre, with the permission of an open-minded manager (Szczesiak, 2000, pp. 34-8).

Because he was able to give accurate health diagnoses, soon people started consulting him informally, and he provided information through psychometry (where information about a person seems to be conveyed through a personal possession belonging to that person). This informal success eventually led to a career as a professional clairvoyant.

His involvement in police work also had informal beginnings, through people hearing about his gift. Once a man turned up on his doorstep, desperate to locate his van, which had been stolen and was essential to his business. The man had reported the theft to the police but they had no success in locating it. Jackowski described in detail the van's location and the appearance of the person who took it; strangely, he could see the young man both with long hair and with his head shaved. The owner of the van immediately recognised the description as his son; a little earlier the lad borrowed the van and forgot to tell his father that he left it at his uncle's place where it was still safely parked, while the young man left to join the unit where he was doing his military service. He used to have long hair but had shaved his head when he was called up.

Case closed; but later after the police had learnt about how it was solved, they asked Jackowski to help find the bodies of two teenagers who had drowned in one of the local lakes. Jackowski asked for clothes and photos, and then located on the map a place next to an island on the lake where there was a very deep ditch and what looked like an underwater spring. The police had been looking for the bodies on the other side of the island where the children had been boating, but the bodies were later found where Jackowski said they were, in the underwater ditch next to the underwater spring. He had described the spot accurately (Świątkowska & Jackowski, 2012, vol, 1 pp. 62-64 & vol. 2 p. 198).

And so his fame grew, with members of the public and police seeking his services. Currently (2022), he seems to be "driven", devoting much of his life to solving cases, which usually involve personal tragedies and/or gruesome events. As mentioned earlier, he keeps letters from various local authorities as well as individuals, thanking him for help in locating bodies of relatives – people whose death was accidental, people with dementia or other mental problems who had wandered off and got lost – others with nobody living knowing who might know where they might have gone to. The letters form an impressive dossier documenting his career. In later chapters we will examine the vast volume of evidence for the existence of clairvoyance – detailed knowledge of objects/events inaccessible to physical senses – and its implications.

There is a long history of experiments with psychics such as the famous Stefan Ossowiecki, as well as large-scale experiments with ordinary people that provide statistical evidence of the phenomenon.

In recent decades we have learnt a great deal from remote viewing experiments, which use highly controlled procedures. However, in the case of Jackowski, we have real-life investigations that have a different context and perspective: they are valid case studies of human stories, often tragic, that are supported by official statements that might not have been solved without Jackowski's input.

In a murder case, Jackowski not only recounted events from the victim's past that led to the murder, but he also identified the murderer, his whereabouts at the time, and advised the police on the best way of obtaining evidence against him. We have the case of a respectable lady who had gone missing, who, it turned out, had committed suicide because she could not bear to be found out in a fraud; in that case Jackowski seems to feel her anguish as well as seeing the exact position of her body. In another case, he is able to track the criminal almost like a dog following a scent, through unknown areas of an unknown city.

There are many cases where he has located dead bodies. Western psychics do it too but western mediums usually try to help the bereaved by seeking information that confirms that their dead loved ones still exist. Jackowski ascribes to the dead a more active role; he feels that it is often the dead who provide him with the information about the location of their corpses and who try to help the living in this way. This is the way he interprets finding people whose bodies for example drifted down rivers. Clearly, this is clairvoyance, but clairvoyance that operates in a specific way. In a culture where there is no tradition of mediumship, the phenomenon is worth looking at more closely, which we will do in later chapters.

The range and extent of information provided clairvoyantly is one of the features that makes Jackowski's dossier unique. His cases are purely qualitative and narrative, but, unlike narratives studied in phenomenological research, where structured interviews are the norm, these narratives can be brief and chaotic. However, they are supported by accounts from different sources, with a timeline clearly demonstrating the impossibility of using normal channels for gathering information.

The statistics regarding his performance are only approximate and not up to date. Jackowski's documentation does not include all cases, nor analysis of degrees of success in specific cases. This is hardly surprising since what he does is not a research project but a way of life, and the recording of cases comes from the police and/or the individuals concerned.

By 2012 he had been contacted by approximately 1500 people and helped in solving more than 1000 cases; around 700 involved looking for missing persons, but there were also missing works of art, documents and animals.

Jackowski feels that when he tries to connect with the "target" he is trying to enter someone else's psyche and, in doing so, is violating his own psyche. That's what makes his work difficult. Every day he feels he owes something to someone and he wakes up every morning feeling guilty. Fortunately, for those of us interested in the evidence for clairvoyance, his insuperable need to demonstrate to the world that clairvoyance does exist wins over such feelings.

He is a psychometrist[2] to the point of total immersion in the psychometric object. He uses photographs or objects, but prefers more personal things such as things that people used to wear. Unusually for a clairvoyant, his "ritual" involves the sense of smell; he handles things, smells them, puts them close to his forehead, and sometimes even puts them on. He regards the smell of the object as one of the keys to the information in the target person's memory, and that is his way of letting it enter his own mind. That is what he is trying to do: to capture its essence, to absorb the other person's energy, and the more the object had been used the better – since it carries the person's unique "energy trace" – a unique code. This is not

---

[2]   As has been said, psychometry is using someone's personal possession as a "guide" to the information about that person.

a metaphorical description; he really does try to use his physical senses to imbue the object with his own energy, to pull the object into himself so that it mixes with his energy and enables him to *become* the person to whom it had belonged. He has to do that to "feel" the person because he or she has to take him to wherever their physical body is. He also thinks that there may be people whose psyche is so different from his that they repel each other (Świątkowska & Jackowski, 2012, vol 1, p. 105; vol. 2, p. 130).

Once he "feels" the person, what they are like, he begins to sense their experience; he gets an image and a feeling. Sometimes he seems to hear the voice of the missing person; sometimes the information comes as if from a bird's eye point of view.

His "visions" or "readings" (there is no adequate term to describe these impressions) do not last long; he may have to wait a long time but the vision itself is usually just a flash, a few seconds, and is very specific. The best, most precise visions come when he does not think and does not concentrate. To focus he needs to be relaxed, and it helps to be among people who are talking and paying no attention to him; his way of encouraging the right state of mind involves seeking distractions and noise. Sometimes he gets cross when he does not "get" the dead; he calls them names, hurls the objects away, and at other times things go very quickly. It seems to depend on the kind of person he is looking for. While the first impressions come spontaneously, the next stage involves reasoning. When he sees the details clearly, he makes a drawing of the area and then uses a map, trying to establish further details, sometimes by looking for likely landmarks (e.g., he "saw" the bodies of two drowned boys in a lake the shape of a kidney, but there were other lakes in the area so more deductive work was required) (Szczesiak, 2000, p. 94).

He does not enter into a trance state, but what sounds like a slightly altered state of consciousness. The state he is trying to achieve is to be focused while calm and relaxed; a kind of tuning in without using logic or reasoning, with an empty mind. He tries to avoid famous cases so as not to fall prey to suggestion; for the same reason he wants to know as little as possible about the cases he takes on.

Originally he regarded his abilities as clairvoyance, but over the years came to the conclusion that the information he obtains comes from those who are no longer alive physically[3]. He realises that his gift and

---

[3] The distinction between clairvoyance and mediumship (defined as contact with the dead) is a familiar concept in psychical research, but not part of Jackowski's cultural background.

the experiences it brings deform his personal life and personality. He becomes chaotic in dealing with everyday matters, nervous when he is working on a case, sometimes for days; he neglects things that matter at the personal level: they simply do not interest him. He becomes quite divorced from reality, and that is not a good thing because then it is difficult to come back to it.

Anomalous phenomena: The media and social reactions

For some years now Jackowski has been working full-time as a clairvoyant, having formed a company called "Parapsychological Services". By the time of writing, alongside his psychic detection, he has a successful career as what might be called a media personality, with talks on his own channel and various publications. He has also given talks about his gift at a number of universities in Poland, devoting much attention to the question of the human soul and its existence after death. He had not started out with this worldview but now he believes that the dead help him. As an example he quotes a case when he was as if "hypnotised" into putting on a dirty shirt brought to him, along with the other belongings of the dead person (known to have drowned); at the time he did not know why he did it, why the shirt felt friendly and why he examined himself in it in the mirror, but now he thinks it was not him but the dead man's soul who wanted to enter his body. Immediately after that experience he knew exactly where to find the body.

He has also taken part in a number of tests. In 2002 he won a clairvoyance competition organised by a television channel in Japan, and a TV channel (Polsat) in Poland produced a series about him while another channel (Canal +) devoted a full-length documentary to him and his activities.

Being famous, he is constantly both attacked and courted by the media. This shapes a lot of his activities as well as his attitudes – he can be difficult, tetchy, opinionated, self-important and bitter – all natural responses to the outside pressures, and of course he is constantly dealing with horrific traumas. When he gets it wrong the fallout can be catastrophic, with feelings of guilt at the personal level for creating unnecessary grief or false hope. He recounts a number of failures in his autobiography (*The dead speak*, Świątkowska & Jackowski, 2012).

When there's a failure the media intensifies the pressure. The press coverage was vitriolic in 2000 after he claimed that a young couple missing in the mountains were dead, and then they turned up alive. On the other hand, he sometimes cooperates with the media by providing predictions of a general nature about world events. Unlike specific cases, general predictions are often difficult to verify and perhaps increase the likelihood of the subject of clairvoyance and Jackowski himself being taken less seriously than is deserved.

There is also a degree of prejudice against him for using his ability as a source of income (although he never charges the police), even though he is open about it, does not charge much, and like most of us, has to make a living somehow.

In a conversation with Janoszka, Jackowski admitted the attacks at times almost drove him to suicide (Janoszka, 2018, pp. 116-125). He is obviously very much aware of the suffering caused when he gets his visions wrong, and that would seem to be pressure enough. According to Robert Bernatowicz (Janoszka, 2014, p. 106), a journalist who researches paranormal stories and who is a long-standing witness to Jackowski's activities, there is a sizeable group of people who have an ideological hatred of him and what he does. These are fundamentalists, both materialist and religious, who verbally attack whenever he is mentioned. He feels these attacks deeply, yet at the same time has an enormous need to keep proving that he has a special gift, and to keep taking up the challenge. It does not help that these days he is also driven to talk about the soul whenever he speaks publicly. This infuriates both groups whose very divergent ways of thinking, pervasive and influential at societal level, tend to converge when it comes to Jackowski. And of course it is more comfortable to identify with a generally accepted point of view, something he commented on in an (unpublished) interview with Janoszka:

> I have often been interviewed on the subject of what might be called the possibility of 'sensing' the soul of a dead person. In such conversations you could always hear a doubt, a form of self-reassurance – as if the journalists wanted to convey something along the lines: 'I am talking to you because the readers are interested in the subject, but we know these are silly things, and I want you to know that I don't believe it, I am an atheist and a sceptic.' ... perhaps we are ashamed to show that we hope for something more than what we see and feel here and now?

The religious opposition to Jackowski's activities and views can be seen as a reaction to the challenge to the authority of the church, regarded by many believers as having a monopoly on things spiritual and supernatural, especially when they concern the soul and contact with the dead. Roman Catholicism is the predominant religion in Poland, and for historical reasons the kind of mediumship practised in other countries of Europe never took hold there.

Why the materialist opposition is a more complex question: why is what Jackowski does such a challenge to mainstream science and opinion that it has to be dismissed, stamped out and erased? Jackowski is one example in a field of anomalistic phenomena that is generally misrepresented and erased, particularly from the biographies of famous people otherwise highly regarded for their achievements in their fields[4]. This reinforces the view of such "anomalies" as a subject not worthy of investigating by respectable scientists. We want to make sense of the world and we rely on science and its figures of authority to give us a general framework of how the world works.

If science tells us that something is impossible we tend to accept it. On the other hand, scientific views and "facts" change over time as new facts falsify the old. Even now, the fundamentals of science are leading us away from naïve physicalism, making room for the study of consciousness in its various forms and pushing the boundaries of knowledge further.

Clairvoyance is an anomaly that does not make sense from a purely physicalist perspective, which is why there is no room in it for Jackowski and others like him. However, there are new directions and developments and other possible worldviews that are becoming acceptable to mainstream science and yet might make room for such phenomena. This is a task for philosophers, but a provisional framework where such things are possible is essential if we want to examine phenomena such as clairvoyance in a systematic way, rather

---

[4] Such as the entry in the Polish Wikipedia for Tadeusz Mieczysław Sokołowski (1887-1965), who throughout the interwar period was actively involved in psychical research in Poland, serving as president or on the board of a number of Warsaw's societies for psychical research that formed over that time. He had an outstanding medical career, received many prestigious awards, but his entry in the Polish Wikipedia totally ignores his interest in the subject. Not surprisingly, Julian Ochorowicz, regarded as the father of Polish psychology, in official biographies is chastised for his aberrant interest in mediumship, while the entry of Poland's science figurehead, Marie Curie-Skłodowska, does not to mention her interest in psychical research and experiments with Palladino.

than as weird and wonderful stories that do not belong in our familiar everyday world.

Let us take a little detour into a very brief and selective history of science and anomalies.

Zofia Weaver
Warsaw 2022

2

SCIENCE, CONSCIOUSNESS, AND ANOMALIES

~

Physics and anomalies

As we learn from studying history, our understanding of the world is a framework of models constructed on the knowledge available at the time. Models of how the world works change over time, sometimes considerably, and they change because of new evidence. That evidence sometimes starts out as persistent anomalies, occurrences that just do not fit into the orderly framework. Ptolemy's model of the universe, which placed the Earth at its centre, was one of a number of models that occurred to ancient Greeks as they contemplated the world around them. This geocentric system coped best with predicting the positions of the planets; it also did very well in guiding navigation, successfully explained the structure of the universe, and so became a dogma and took root in religion. And so, for some 1400 years (from the 2nd to the 16th century), for most of recorded history, this was the mainstream view. There were plenty of anomalies but they were unimportant enough to be ignored; yet it was the effort of recording and measuring persistent anomalies that eventually forced a change to the mainstream model. It replaced the Earth with the Sun at the centre of the universe, causing religious and philosophical upheaval in the process. There was a heavy price to be paid for going against the dogma, which is perhaps why neither Copernicus nor Galileo rushed to support heliocentrism in public, however much they contributed to establishing its veracity in private. New ideas need time to become accepted, especially when they go not only against the entrenched views, but also against the common-sense view that is formed by observing the reality around us (such as the Sun travelling across the sky).

The successful march of enlightenment that has brought us the modern world relied on the gradual acceptance of the view that measurement and observation are at the core of science. By the 19th century Newtonian physics, or classical mechanics, became king of natural sciences[5], and the industrial revolution, reliant on technological progress, drew on the model of physics. Chemistry and biology, the natural sciences, were and still are seen as deriving from physics, that most fundamental of sciences. These sciences followed physics in being concerned with the objective, outside world, experimenting with it and measuring it with increasing accuracy. On the other hand consciousness, understood as a subjective, individual experience, did not lend itself to being measured, and during most of the 19th century psychology was a concern of philosophy, not science. Subjective consciousness had no place in science; it was outside the domain of physics in a world driven by mechanistic forces. The phrase "physics envy" is sometimes applied in criticisms of modern psychology when it tries to quantify the varieties of human experience. Integrating subjective consciousness into science (let alone extrasensory perception!) seems, in some ways, to require a revolution on a similar scale as the one that took us from geocentrism to heliocentrism.

However, anomalies have a way of producing revolutions by persistently subverting the prevalent worldview. This is what happened to physics: just when it seemed that all that was needed was more measurement with better accuracy, anomalies turned the mechanistic world on its head, at the turn of the 19th and 20th centuries, with quantum mechanics and relativity. This did not mean that consciousness came onto the physics agenda (even though Max Planck, the originator of quantum mechanics, regarded it as fundamental) as a subject of investigation, but it did mean that the world turned out to be a very weird place and not the predictable clockwork mechanism it had been

---

[5] From the title of history of 19th century physics, *When physics became king* (2005) by I.R. Morus. The queen of science is mathematics.

assumed to be. And this topsy-turvy world produced an influx of new ideas in an effort to account for its strangeness.

Even if we know little about physics, we have probably gathered that it is now notorious for arguments about fundamental things that turn out not to be fundamental: dark matter and dark energy being an obvious example of unknowns that seem to occupy most of our universe yet are only a recent discovery. We understand that quantum mechanics underlies the classical, Newtonian model, that the smallest bits of the universe behave differently from the even slightly bigger objects; for many of us, that is as far as our knowledge extends. But physics itself evolves and produces new models that may mean worldview revolutions on the same scale as the one that revolutionised the Newtonian universe. Matter can behave in unexpected ways (as in the well-known experiment when cooled helium becomes superfluid, climbs walls and leaks out of leak-free containers) and its new phases are being discovered in the search for new technologies. There is now talk of fields that fill the whole universe, a bubbling broth of interactive fields of constantly forming and unforming bits of matter. And so, in this view, fundamentally, matter seems to boil down to excitations and undulations bubbling away in a quantum pot.

Yet, in sufficient numbers, these undulations seem to organise themselves into structures and processes. More *is* different[6], and when we have more we look for patterns, and then we construct our natural laws from these patterns. More complex structures emerge from simpler ones, and form wholes that transcend their parts. Thanks to science, and largely thanks to this approach, our models discover an increasingly complex universe, demonstrating their incompleteness.

How did the universe come to be the way it is? We have not mentioned time yet; for Newton, it ticked away smoothly in the background without relation to anything external, and most of us do not move fast enough to be troubled by Einstein's time equation. Yet there is a profound debate in physics about the nature of time. Is it only a measure of change, relevant to us but irrelevant to the universe as a whole, or is it fundamental to creating space and everything in it, a network of relationships that evolve, with laws of nature emerging in time, changing and leading to increased complexity (Smolin, 2019; Rovelli, 2018)?

---

[6]   *More is different* is the title of a famous article by Paul Anderson, arguing that "at each level of complexity entirely new properties appear" ... "At each stage entirely new laws, concepts and generalizations are necessary" (Anderson, 1972, p. 393).

There is a plethora of different theories and models in physics, including other dimensions and universes, that reflect our awareness of the incompleteness of our knowledge. It also involves that other great unknown: consciousness. A number of outstanding physicists recognised that physics is incomplete without accommodating consciousness. James Jeans described the universe as "a great thought"; John Wheeler famously coined the phrase "it from bit" (information as the basis of physics); Max Planck and Erwin Schrödinger argued that universe is mind-like, while some physicists of the John von Neumann-Eugene Wigner school of thought claim that the mind of a conscious observer is necessary to produce quantum measurement (begging the question of what constitutes such a mind). However, even when such incompleteness is recognised, this does not translate into the kinds of definitions and formulae that science can work with. The current physical theories do not include or predict the existence of consciousness.

Physics describes a world where there is no inner reality and no subjective experience. It does not need to include consciousness in the description of the measurable world of objectively observable properties. And, obviously, unlike in the case of matter, we have not found a way of measuring consciousness (as opposed to brain activity, which of course neuroscience measures with ever-increasing precision).

Where does consciousness fit in?

In philosophy and the sciences there are many nuanced discussions of consciousness, its definitions and its role. However, at a level that we all understand, consciousness can be described as subjective experience and in that respect the most prevalent current mainstream view seems to be that consciousness is an emergent property associated with the workings of the brain. This means that at some level of complexity, previously non-existent properties emerge from the new, more complex system. For some strict materialists even this is going too far[7]; for others, such as the zoologist Matthew Cobb, such emergence is "often our only resort", since "the gulf between physical and mental phenomena remains as yawning as it was to Leibniz in the eighteenth century". On this view, we can find

---

[7] For extreme epiphenomenalists, mental experience is an irrelevant byproduct of physical events in the body – in fact, an anomaly.

a parallel between emergent consciousness in living beings and "the amazing properties of deep learning programs" in artificial intelligence, which develop properties beyond the understanding of the people who designed them (Cobb, 2020, p.361, 375). The basic components of hardware and software in combination produce unexpected results and, by extension and analogy, neural networks, with their chemical and electrical interactions, at some point became sufficiently complex to somehow produce subjective experience; this is the core understanding of consciousness in many mainstream discussions without any need to postulate non-physical components.

Subjective experience all the way down?

However, there is a problem here. Much of consciousness and neuroscientific research is concerned with the activities of human brains, yet much of what we are and what forms us is common to all living creatures, and not limited to the chemical/electrical activity of the human brain. Subjective experience is not exclusive to humans; it happens to all living organisms, even the simplest ones as they interact with the environment in a variety of ways, down to the bacteria in our gut and the cells in our bodies. "Ingenious, perceptive and intelligent behaviour is apparent in a single living cell" (McGilchrist, 2021, p. 746). Maxine Sheets-Johnstone argues that proprioperception – awareness of the body's position and movement – is the starting point of consciousness. Bacteria rely on sensing their own energy to determine the direction of their movement, which "strongly suggests how a form of corporeal consciousness is present in bacteria" in monitoring the environment. Sophisticated sensory perception, with external and internal sensors, is part of our evolved, layered corporeal consciousness, and we share it with nonhuman animals. Our sensory mechanisms are specific to our species, but interacting with the environment and self-awareness, in the sense of being driven by the need to ensure survival, seem to be an integral part of life. "Know thyself" is incontrovertibly a fundamental biological built-in. This tends to be forgotten as philosophers and neuroscientists become "mesmerised by brains", ignoring human rootedness in the "creaturely world" (Sheets-Johnstone, 1998). Living systems act on the information they learn and remember about themselves and their environment: in other words they assign meanings to events and have intentionality, however limited their scale. In this sense all life is conscious and the subjective experience that is unique to the individual (the "qualia" of philosophy) is not an illusion. "Small brains are now known to produce behaviours that look very similar to those produced by our own, from perception and learning through excitement, indecision, prediction, foresight, aggression, personality and responding to pain" (Cobb, 2020, p. 386). We are mindful bodies as much as embodied minds, and from that perspective the claim "I feel therefore I am" is more accurate than defining consciousness in terms of sophisticated reasoning skills. It thus makes sense to see ourselves as part of a continuum, with "emotion or something very much like it ... driving evaluative sensory motor behavior toward that which is "good for me" and away from that which is "bad for me" (Kauffman-Peil, 2015 p. 15). Self-awareness, a sense of "I/not-I", however rudimentary, is essential for responding appropriately to the environment, as is emotion, "an attitude" to the incoming messages, giving them a meaning. Viewed in this way, it is indeed consciousness all the way down, but such a sense of continuity, of universal connection, is not reductive – on the contrary, it creates a context for examining human consciousness, the selves that we create throughout our lives – and the degrees of awareness and interaction with the environment they are capable of. It also means that we do not know to what extent that which we regard as anomalies applies to the rest of the living world.[8]

So, we now know that, as living systems, we share with other mammals many of the more sophisticated biochemicals that influence our emotions, our various neurotransmitters. Structures with the same functions as parts of our brains are found in other species. We begin our lives as foetuses with no perceptible personal identity – we grow a body – and as we do, we also grow a self. That self consists of various strands: emotions, thoughts, memories, imagination, personality traits, dreams and states of awareness. The strands cohere, integrate, persist and change over time. They can also be damaged or enhanced through effects on the body, through illness, drugs, diet or environment, since the self ingests experiences through the senses, the body and the brain. But it is these strands that create our sense of identity, our self; the self is the experiencer, the continuous flow of "experiential

---

[8] The obvious example is provided by Rupert Sheldrake's research into *Dogs that know when their owners are coming home* (Sheldrake, 2011); research into other species may reveal other, less familiar aspects of consciousness.

continuity" irrespective of any changes to physical states. This is what we understand by consciousness in everyday life: to use an old but valid definition of "self"[9]: "an individual regarded as conscious of his own continuing identity and of his relation to the environment". According to the philosopher Barry Dainton "you do not cease to exist as streams of consciousness when you 'become' Napoleon [in a virtual reality setting]; it is *experiential continuity*, not psychological continuity (...) that is of paramount importance." (Dainton, p. 61). It is that level of consciousness, or highly "integrated information", that is now part of scientific discourse as a legitimate aspect of complex living systems, not necessarily just human.

Information and consciousness

The difficulty in accounting for subjective experience and self-awareness has been described as the "hard problem"[10]. There has been tremendous progress in the study of the "easy problem", finding neural correlates of consciousness in humans by objective measurement of neural activity corresponding to the "reportable knowledge" provided by people engaged in particular tasks. However, knowledge of how aspects of a person's brain (or indeed any creature's organs of perception) might be involved in processing particular information involved in an experience does not translate into knowledge of that individual's experience. This has led a number of philosophers and scientists to propose that consciousness should be regarded as fundamental: if something cannot be explained with the existing fundamentals, one has to look for its own fundamental laws. Neuroscientists such as Christoph Koch and Giulio Tononi, physicists such as Vlatko Vedral and Federico Faggin and psychologists such as Donald Hoffman, all describe consciousness in slightly different ways, but use terms such as universal, primary, elementary or fundamental, immanent in complex systems. For Koch and Tononi (Koch, 2017, 2019, 2021; Tononi & Koch, 2015), consciousness is an elementary aspect of living matter, which cannot be derived from anything or explained through the existing (physical) fundamental properties. According to them, properly formulated information theory

---

[9] I owe this definition to Alan Gauld (Gauld, 2022, p. 298); it comes from *Howard Warren's Dictionary of Psychology (1935)*.

[10] The concept defined by David Chalmers (Chalmers, 1996).

will identify the essential properties of consciousness *per se*. This means that these properties should be examined independently of the activities of brains, because information is "substrate-independent". Transferring the "mind" to some electronic device is a far-fetched idea for many reasons but it reflects our awareness that, in a fundamental physical sense, we are arrangements of particles, many of them replaced over time, yet our sense of personal identity continues over that time. The earlier and later person carries an awareness of their experiences (not necessarily consciously), and memories are dependent on the earlier experiences. Seen in this way, consciousness exists, is irreducible to physical properties, and has properties of its own, its own structure, complexity and degrees of integration (varying in different living species)[11].

Such a view of consciousness, that there is a sense of purpose at the biological level, and that life experiences modify genetic inheritance ("the epigenetic tail wagging the genetic dog"), once dismissed as heresy, is now returning as science re-examines the role that information plays in the creation and evolution of life. We now talk of self-organisation, self-regulation, biosemiotics (signs and codes in biology), bioinformatics, about information being the opposite of entropy and having causal powers, thus allowing organisms to have a hand (so to speak) in their own evolution. Paul Davies talks of a new scientific field whose unifying concept is "*information,* not in its prosaic everyday sense but as an abstract quantity, which, like energy, has the ability to animate matter" (Davies, 2019, p. 129, p.2). This view, that brings consciousness into the picture as one of the main components of life, is a very significant departure from Francis Crick's famous definition of humanity, "you are nothing but a pack of neurons".

For a long time, for much of the 20th century, ignoring subjective experience was the approach adopted by mainstream psychology to the awkward problem it presented. Consciousness would not fit into the ideal scientific procedure of objective measurement, and that was an obstacle to mainstream psychology's becoming a proper empirical science, distinct from the vague musings of philosophy on such unmeasurable topics as the nature and meaning of life or ethics.

---

[11] Such a way of solving the problem of the relationship between the mind (self) and the body moves towards panpsychism, where everything, down to the smallest particles, has the potential for a tiny degree of information/consciousness.

The version of psychology that tried to delve into the depths of human psyche through examining subjective experience was pushed aside, dismissed as attempts to investigate an epiphenomenon, an irrelevant by-product of the mechanical workings of the brain. The dominant scientific approach was behaviourism, which saw psychology as an investigation of observable and measurable responses of organisms to environmental stimuli, rejecting inner mental (or indeed physiological) experience. This has since given way to a number of approaches and ideas that recognise the complexity of the phenomenon of consciousness; cognitive neuroscience, the study of complex biological processes that underlie organisms' responses to the environment, is perhaps the most influential aspect of modern psychology. But for some this now takes into account the role that information plays at every level, from DNA to social organization (Davies, 2019, p.2).

Anomalies beyond the pale

It seems that a new scientific paradigm is being formed, one that makes space for life and consciousness that were anomalous in a mechanistic view of the basic sciences. Scientific investigation of anomalies, whatever their nature, is a recognised and fruitful approach that gives insights into aspects that a normally functioning organism or system does not usually display but are there all the same. Perhaps we are now seeing mainstream science progressing to a better understanding of complex phenomena through investigating aspects that seemed irrelevant or "rogue" until a new theoretical approach emerged.

However, this approach does not (as yet) extend to taking account of phenomena as "rogue" as psi[12], the extraordinary human experiences investigated by psychical research and parapsychology that did not develop as part of mainstream psychology. The evidence for them, like the evidence which overturned geocentrism, consists of anomalies that persistently turn up and cause frictions in the established worldview. They have been observed and recorded for centuries; they have been collected, investigated and experimented with for more than a century,

---

[12] Generally speaking, "psi" is the term covering phenomena that involve consciousness acting without the use of the physical senses. I prefer this wider term than "extrasensory perception", which implies passive reception when more seems to be involved even in simple tests.

and by now present a sizeable body of data. But they just do not fit in, however hard we try to bring them into the mainstream in which consciousness is understood as permanently and closely tied to a physical substratum.

Parapsychologists tend to turn to physics when trying to find a place where a theory of psi might fit. Indeed, psi should eventually fit in with one or more of the evolving landscapes in physics. However, since physics itself seems to be in a state of flux and awaiting a higher, more transcendent level of understanding, it seems unlikely that using concepts, which themselves need clarification, will help our understanding of psi.

Lawrence LeShan regretted being one of the first to suggest investigating psi at the level of quantum physics, because "dignity, love, loyalty, awe, and psi must be dealt with on their own terms in a science built on these observables, not one built on the observables of subatomic particles." (LeShan, 2009, p. 15). He also made the very reasonable point that different laws, different basic limiting principles, apply to different segments or levels of reality.

Concepts such as entanglement and non-locality (or what Einstein described as "spooky action at a distance", with correlated particles being linked in spite of the distance between them), when used away from physics are certainly good metaphors[13], effective in conveying the direction of travel, but do not provide insights into the workings of phenomena such as clairvoyance (awareness of information not available to the five senses). The observer effect in quantum mechanics, the notion that particles come into being when they are "collapsed" into reality by observation, is another idea that at this stage can only function as a metaphor for a hypothesis. And, clearly, the proposed routes to an explanation of consciousness via physics deal with the possible "how" and not "what". Such, for example, is the Penrose-Hameroff hypothesis, where consciousness is an intrinsic feature of the universe, and where signals representing information travel along microtubules – tiny polymers present in all living organisms including humans – transmitting information of varying complexity. Here we have a universal mechanism for achieving consciousness but still no satisfactory definition of what we mean by consciousness, even if we

---

[13] This is not a criticism of the use of metaphors, often the only way to express inexpressible concepts; rather, it is a criticism of using metaphors to cover gaps between ideas from different fields of learning.

know what it is – unavoidably, since it is our multi-level experience of the world and ourselves.

Our notions of mind and matter are in a continuous state of flux, so it may be premature to try to shoehorn the less well understood phenomena of human consciousness into hypotheses from other fields such as physics. The more humble but quite productive approach adopted here is to act as simple "parapsychological naturalists", to borrow a phrase from the philosopher Stephen Braude (Braude, 2019): to collect specimens, to focus on observing and analysing them and their environments, and not to over-theorise. This approach frees us from the presuppositions as to what is and is not possible, with arbitrary cut-off points, before examining the evidence. It seems particularly important in the area of anomalous and extraordinary human experiences.

Psychical research and parapsychology: a little history.

Scientific research into anomalous human experiences, including evidence for the survival of human personality after physical death, has been going on for nearly one hundred and fifty years. It has created a vast area of knowledge that is largely unfamiliar both to mainstream science and to the general public. The evidence is both experimental and observational, some of it supported in ways that meet all the standards of established scientific methodology (although, for obvious reasons, the question of whether there is life – consciousness – after death can only be explored through indirect observation).

The first learned society to undertake investigations into extraordinary human experiences on a regular basis was the Society for Psychical Research (SPR), founded in London in 1882 by a group of prominent scholars. Its purpose was to apply scientific methodology to investigating the phenomena now described as paranormal. The current definitions of the main areas of investigation, not necessarily accurate but in general use, include: Extrasensory Perception (ESP), an umbrella term for telepathy (direct mind-to-mind communication), clairvoyance (awareness of information unavailable through normal sensory channels) and precognition (foreseeing the future); interactions which affect the environment or other organisms physically are referred to as psychokinesis (PK). Large-scale physical disturbances (macro-PK), which occur spontaneously and are generally referred to as poltergeists (from the German meaning 'mischievous spirit'), have also been described as

RSPK (recurrent spontaneous psychokinesis), while micro-PK, involving minute effects, is and has been the subject of a number of experimental studies, including experiments in healing. Both ESP and PK are frequently subsumed under the more general term **psi**. Over the years we have gained a great deal of knowledge about many aspects of these phenomena, particularly those which can be investigated in experimental conditions.

One of the main initial goals of early researchers was to examine scientifically the evidence for the survival of human spirit beyond physical death.

The background to this research was the spread of the idea of evolution. With the publication of Darwin's *On the Origin of Species* in 1859, evolution came to be regarded with good reason as the true and scientific explanation of the origin of mankind. We are now capable of interpreting this idea in ways which accommodate all kinds of worldviews, but at the time it was often seen both by its proponents and enemies as a shocking assault on religion and man's position in the universe. It demoted humanity from its unique position, as God's special creation, to one of nature's accidental productions among many other creatures, and it seemed that the triumph of science left the world bereft of spiritual depth.

But at the other, much less scientifically exalted end of human experience, and very much at the same time, there developed the new religion of Spiritualism. It was based on the idea that one could communicate with the spirits of the dead through specially gifted persons – mediums – and that spirits could produce messages by using physical movement of objects or through knocking on furniture, most commonly little tables. It is usual to date the beginnings of Spiritualism to 1848, when some strange raps produced by young girls (the Fox sisters) in America were interpreted as messages from the departed spirit of a murder victim. Spiritualism and its phenomena have a clear a link to the spontaneous poltergeist reports (or macro-PK) that go back centuries and are still regularly reported today; they also have a long history of being attributed to spirits or demons[14]. The same applies to reports of extraordinary phenomena produced by saints, healers, shamans and other individuals with special gifts. However, what was important for the development of the scientific approach to the question of survival was the new religion's focus on the mediating being, the person with special gifts – the medium.

---

[14] SPR's online *Psi Encyclopedia* is a good place to start exploring the vast literature devoted to physical phenomena.

The craze for "raising spirits" through sittings with mediums or private "table-tipping" séances started in the USA and quickly spread throughout the Western world. There is a great deal of good evidence for anomalous physical phenomena being produced by people under certain conditions, regardless of how one interprets their meaning. However, the popularity of the new religion and the new pastime, and the material advantages which could be gained from them, inevitably attracted a great many fake mediums and bogus claims. Thus, much of the early work of the Society for Psychical Research was a learning curve of detecting and unmasking fraudulent claims. It was undoubtedly excellent apprenticeship in honing a methodology suited to the subject, but the result was that physical mediumship came to be viewed with suspicion. On the other hand, for mental mediumship, i.e., messages allegedly obtained from deceased persons by mediums in altered states of consciousness, produced, under conditions precluding fraud, there is much evidence that remains at least puzzling if not irrefutable.

It was the first collection of spontaneous cases that formed the pinnacle of the Society's early activities. *Phantasms of the Living*, published in 1886, contained over 700 cases. The authors[15] made every effort to corroborate the reports, which included spontaneous and experimental or semi-experimental telepathy, the special role of dreams, clairvoyance, premonitions and apparitions, particularly those relating to crisis, often at or near the moment of death. The thoroughness of the research and the authors' awareness of the need to exclude natural explanations meant that this collection is still an extremely valuable resource for research.

Spontaneous cases are the real-life phenomena which scientific theories of psi seek to explain. Since the beginning of serious research into the paranormal, field investigations were and continue to be carried out and volumes of collections, analyses and surveys of spontaneous phenomena continue to be published. By now they come from different periods and cultures and demonstrate patterns, which are difficult to dismiss. But the challenge of spontaneous cases is that they are not repeatable and are susceptible to all kinds of errors of observation and reporting. For this reason, since the earliest days of research, efforts

---

[15] Many editions of *Phantasms of the Living* by Edmund Gurney, Frederic Myers and Frank Podmore have now been published, and pdf formats are also available online.

were made to devise controlled and quantifiable experiments, which could be applied to larger populations.

The "coming of age" of psychical research as a reputable branch of science seemed set to arrive with the establishment of the Parapsychology Laboratory at Duke University in North Carolina, USA, in the 1930s under the leadership of Dr Joseph Banks Rhine. The Laboratory was committed to the science of 'parapsychology', a strictly experimental approach using large numbers of ordinary people as subjects and simple standard protocols. Subjects were tested for ESP using a card-guessing procedure (Zener cards, invented by a colleague of Rhine, Karl Zener, consisted of five simple symbols in decks of 25 cards), while testing for PK employed dice, where the subjects tried to vary, through mental influence, the frequency of the designated target face. The experiments were transparent and quantifiable using statistical methods in general use; it was thus expected that, employed on a large scale, their results would lead to establishing psi as a universal property, and parapsychology as an academically respectable branch of science. However, in spite of achieving statistically significant results, with independent replications at different laboratories, there was no general acceptance of this new field of knowledge. Since then, many new kinds of experiments and methodologies have been devised, such as creating free response targets with rich content instead of repetitive card guessing, shielding the subjects of experiments from irrelevant stimuli (ganzfeld), and automating much of the experimental process which ensures randomness and eliminates the possibility of fraud. Many of the results are "methodologically sound and statistically significant" (Broughton, 2015), and since 1969 the Parapsychology Association, the professional organisation of researchers in this field, has been a member of the prestigious American Association for the Advancement of Science.

Indeed, parapsychology has become an academic subject in some countries, with various projects carried out by eminent academics or as part of postgraduate research. However, it is still regarded with suspicion as "pseudoscience" by much of the mainstream. It is not just a question of ignorance of the body of evidence, although this is a problem. A much greater problem is that the evidence for psi, if accepted, challenges the established assumptions about how the world works. What makes this evidence particularly troublesome is that it is based on methods and techniques recognised as legitimately scientific. Any positive results thus represent a challenge, unlike the humanities where literature, religion or anything to do with the human spirit can safely be compartmentalised as belief systems and social constructs, with domains of their own. For example: when a highly regarded mainstream psychologist Daryl Bem (Bem, 2011), obtained positive results in experiments in precognition using standard psychological methods in reverse[16] and had his results published in a reputable journal, the response was vitriolic. Some questioned the validity of the standard methodology itself; the journal was severely criticised for publishing the paper even though it was methodologically flawless, and even unsuccessful, let alone successful, replications were refused publication. One article summed up the general judgment on Bem's research as "both methodologically sound and logically insane" (Engber, 2017).

When research by eminent academics employing standard methodology under laboratory conditions is dismissed out of hand because it appears to challenge dogma, clearly a mainstream career in investigating "anomalous" aspects of human experience is difficult. One way of dealing with the problem has been to talk around the phenomenon, approaching it from a social and/or psychological perspective; another involves changing the subject's name (such as anomalous cognition or extraordinary experience), or exploring the possible benefits of paranormal beliefs for mental healthcare. Such "respectable" approaches are undoubtedly of value, but they do not deal with the basic questions of the extent and function of psi. It seems that the evidence of parapsychology, some of it beyond methodological reproach, is an academic non-starter.

Sometimes this attitude is attributed to the absence of theoretical framework, but this is not the only field where there is no "grand unified theory" yet research goes on unchallenged. In some ways parapsychology also falls between two stools: reports of people's spontaneous experiences are dismissed as anecdotal, however universal and common they might

---

[16] For example, reversing the procedure for tests for subliminal influence. One such experiment is where participants are exposed to stimuli such as words so briefly that they are not aware of them consciously, but when shown these words afterwards among other words for long enough to register consciously, they respond to them more quickly. In some of Bem's experiments the participants were shown the subliminal stimuli randomly selected by the computer *after* they had made their conscious choices during testing, but reacted during the tests as if they had already been influenced by them (i.e., more quickly), challenging our expectation that in a well-ordered world causes must precede effects.

be, and sometimes they are also latched onto by simplistic belief systems (not to mention crude representations in the media) which quite justifiably raise scientific eyebrows. On the other hand, the vehement refusal even to examine experimental evidence by mainstream science is probably a defensive posture that makes sense: once you accept the results of, for example, card-guessing experiments as valid, however mainstream their design, you open doors to the idea that "subjects can be *aware* in some sense of physical states of affairs ... whose sensory perception ordinarily requires being suitably situated in space" (Braude, 2020, p. 206). In other words, there is no physical position from which one could "peer" at the card. And that "logically insane" idea undercuts the physicalist worldview at its foundations, using the tools of science to boot.

Properly carried out experiments should be acceptable as scientific evidence contributing to our knowledge. However, in experiments one only tests what can be tested and controlled, and mainstream experimentation sometimes means using methodologies that may be inappropriate in the context of something as elusive as psi, but are acceptable to the academic establishment. With funding limited and the threat to institutional and individual academic reputations posed by simply being associated with the subject, research being carried out in this field is miniscule. While there have been some very promising lines of research, such as dream ESP, they are usually not followed on a larger scale, and the effects of small-scale experiments can often be erratic since what they test is variable even in the same humans under the same external conditions.

In spite of these limitations, a great deal has been achieved by the experimental approach to the subject. We have learned about the importance of altered states of consciousness in creating conditions conducive to psi (such as the ganzfeld technique aimed at reducing the subject's sensory input), as well as the importance of belief in/ expectation of success (the "sheep-goats effect" where the "sheep" score above chance on psi tasks while "goats" score below it). Of even greater importance has been a better if not full understanding of the possibility of experimenter effect, where one has to disentangle the possible psi coming from the researcher, the influence of the researcher's attitude, and that on top of the variables pertaining to the participants. The experimenter effect has been noted in various areas of learning, but is particularly relevant to parapsychology.

Perhaps progress in acceptance of the subject as a scientific endeavour is being made. Recently an article by Etzel Cardeña, who is Thorsen professor of psychology at Lund University in Sweden, was published in a mainstream psychology journal. The article makes the case for psi evidence, based on the changing worldviews in physics and purely experimental evidence, mainly produced during the recent decades. It quotes meta-analyses of various kinds of experiments with significant psi effects that could not be dismissed with claims of "sensory leakage, recording or intentional errors, selective reporting, multiple analyses of variables, failures in randomization or statistical errors, and independence of studies". In fact, psi research was found in some respects to be more rigorous than psychology research in general. (Cardeña, 2018, p. 11). Cardeña makes the important point that the requirement to replicate performance "on demand" is also unrealistic in relation to ordinary psychology studies, which face the same problems, since dealing with human beings involves too many variables for which one cannot control.

The databases which showed most consistent statistically significant results included the ganzfeld experiments (where participants are put in a relaxed state with some degree of sensory deprivation), presentiment experiments (where participants' physical responses are recorded and show arousal prior to being shown a stimulus), precognition, dream research into telepathy (particularly in the famous Maimonides Medical Center sleep laboratory, where participants selected for psychic ability were woken up every time after they had been in REM sleep and had their dreams recorded), remote viewing (clairvoyance experiments with strict protocols), and even forced choice (the boring Zener cards) experiments. On the PK side, significant results were obtained in influencing the fall of dice or skewing results produced by Random Event Generators, as well as various forms of healing (e.g., intention affecting biological tissue or whole living beings) and the staring experiments (people being aware of being stared at even though the "starer" is isolated from them) made famous by Rupert Sheldrake. Most of these effects were small but the methodology was sound, and it may be the case that adversity, in the form of general academic hostility to the subject, helped to hone research practice by the few determined individuals who never gave up. All that data tells us that the ability to be psychic is latent in at least a large proportion of the population, can be expected to be greater in certain types of personalities and can be encouraged by providing conditions conducive to psi success. It is reassuring that psi is not a totally "freaky", unpredictable thing that science cannot cope with even if, like any human activity, it is not totally reliable.

But there are also now relatively new areas of psi research, and some of them have implications for renewing scientific research even into the possibility of survival of bodily death. We owe progress in these areas to science: one area is the medical sciences, where modern resuscitation methods allow people to be saved from death and recount their experiences while they were clinically dead (at the same time raising questions about the definition of clinical death). Such near-death accounts go back to antiquity, but it is only in the last three decades that a sizeable volume of such accounts has been produced, many of them taking place in hospital settings and verified by medical staff (Holden et al., 2009, Hagan 2017). From another perspective, research into mediumship, while not new, is now benefitting from new technologies that allow one to eliminate some of the difficulties which beleaguered it in previous times, such as leakage of information through physical means. Also, reports of past life recall indicating reincarnation have been with us for centuries and come from virtually all cultures, but the volume of cases and the quality of background research would not have been achievable without modern technologies.

Thus, on the one hand we have consistent, small-scale statistically significant experiments, limited by having to test that which is testable and fits into the researchers' methodological framework; on the other we have reports of amazing feats which involve apparitions, premonitions, visions, unworldly interventions, and are limited by their one-off, uncorroborated and often private nature. Cardeña rightly observed that, "As compared with real-life circumstances, psi experiments involve impersonal stimuli of little or no consequence, in contrast with reputed psi phenomena observed in everyday life" (Cardeña, 2018, p.10), such as immediate knowledge of the unexpected death of a close person at a distant location. At the same time, individuals with the gift of spectacular psi are few.

Louisa Rhine, wife of J.B. Rhine, thought that collecting spontaneous cases would help to define the boundaries of psi as a complement to experimental research. However, what has happened is that if anything, the gap between experimental and spontaneous evidence has grown bigger. Part of the problem is the very nature of testing. While throughout history there have been a number of gifted psychics, when they are tested they have to fit into the framework of the test. For example, one of the famous star subjects of J.B. Rhine card tests, Pavel Stepanek, could make correct guesses about thousands of coloured cards, but we do not know what else he was capable of achieving. This applies to a number of "psi virtuosi", such as Matthew Manning, a British healer whose childhood involved well-attested poltergeist phenomena and haunting. He participated in numerous successful experiments but stopped because he became bored with having to repeat the same "trick", like influencing compass needles, and not having his gift tested to its limits. (Manning, 1978, p. 2)

Something like 70% of documented experiments with Stefan Ossowiecki, famous Polish clairvoyant[17], involved deciphering concealed writing or drawing through sealed envelopes, and the actual number of such experiments, formal and informal, must have been in the hundreds. We would never know what feats of clairvoyance he was capable of in other ways if it were not for corroborated reports where his skills were employed to solve real-life problems, such as locating missing persons (Barrington et al., 2005). And we would perhaps be more likely to look askance at these reports were it not for the very similar amazing feats of the remote viewers employed by the US military under impeccable conditions (May & Marwaha, 2018). Such feats should not lead us to devalue the significance of card guessing, reading messages in sealed envelopes or, indeed skewing the fall of dice in PK experiments and other repetitive efforts. They may not capture the imagination – they are poorer in individual features – but they are aspects of the same mysterious phenomenon. Once you eliminate fraud, leakage and other "usual suspects" (Stephen Braude's oft-used phrase), you come up against the impossibility of identifying the target through decks of cards or sealed packages using any of the familiar senses.

There is, thus, a continuum between experimental and spontaneous, as well as experimental and volitional evidence, perhaps greater than statistical data can reveal. According to an in-depth analysis by Ed Kelly, Research Professor at the University of Virginia Division of Perceptual Studies, "the gifted subject BD [Bill Delmore] produced in one week of formal testing at the Rhine lab, ... results that are statistically more or less equivalent to that entire thirty-year history of ganzfeld research" (Kelly, in Presti ed. 2018, p. 107). So it makes sense to focus on gifted subjects, but observing them in situations where the results of their efforts are not dissolved in general data, and where real life provides the motivation. If we want to explore the extent of psi we need evidence

---

[17] See the entry in the SPR *Psi Encyclopedia* for basic information on Ossowiecki, perhaps the most famous clairvoyant of the interwar period (Weaver, 2021).

that combines the impressive quality of spontaneous cases and the reliability of experimental evidence. One way of approaching this task is to examine corroborated, competent reports that form consistent repeating patterns in real life situations.

In this context, reports of clairvoyance are of particular interest; many of them have a practical aim, and, for that reason, tend to be well-attested and trustworthy (you cannot have leakage of information if nobody involved or even living has that information). Psychic detection is one aspect of this practical application of clairvoyance. Clearly, clairvoyance itself implies that consciousness can extend beyond the reach of physical senses; however, in some cases, psychic detection seems to involve obtaining information from those no longer living. If claims like this turn out to be based on sound evidence, we live in a world that is very different from what we assume it to be.

3

CONSCIOUSNESS AND CLAIRVOYANCE – A TENTATIVE FRAMEWORK

~

Why evidence needs a framework: expanding the concept of consciousness

However well documented and verified the evidence, if there is no theoretical framework in which it fits somewhere, it ends up ignored, vilified (as were Bem's experiments in presentiments), or categorised as part of a belief system (mainstream religious or fringe). We have no general (let alone mainstream) theoretical framework for a worldview that includes clairvoyance, but we do have evidence suggesting that psi in all its aspects may be a necessary component of life rather than occasional anomalous "supernatural", or miraculous, breakdowns of normality. That evidence does not seem to conflict with much of what mainstream science already tells us about consciousness, so perhaps we can construct a tentative framework (rather than a fully-fledged theory) with an extended, evidence-based view of consciousness.

What do we mean by consciousness extending beyond the physical senses in clairvoyance? Conscious beings acquire information, exchange it and exercise volition, intent; in other words they communicate with each other and with the environment and try to influence both. The question is: are these achievable through means other than physical action (ignoring technology in this instance)?

We have evidence, both experimental and real-life, that information in living systems has causal powers on many levels. Conscious experience driven by volition can be involved in shaping the brain, producing physical differences by sustained thoughts (as in the famous study of London taxi drivers with their enlarged part of the brain devoted to navigation). Specific mental imagery, the intention to act, produces the same neuromuscular patterns as action; sportsmen use mental rehearsals, stroke victims are encouraged to imagine moving their limbs as an aid to recovery, and of course we are all aware of psychosomatic illnesses. The placebo/nocebo effect (where belief in the efficacy of a remedy produces a physical health effect) is very much an accepted part of scientific trials, but its implications in terms of causal powers of belief are not generally discussed outside psychical research (Kelly et al, 2009). Going beyond the more common evidence we have the equally well attested evidence of the body changing under the influence of mental events in stigmata, in experiments in hypnosis and, importantly, in distant healing where the intention of the healer makes a measurable difference even in the case of animals and plants (Charman, 2021). If consciousness is able to influence physical systems at a distance, without sensory contact, then communicating (informing, influencing) must also take place on a fundamental level, not reliant on physical connections.

The unconscious as part of consciousness

Much of what happens in our consciousness goes on beyond our awareness. Ian McGilchrist puts it well in his groundbreaking book *The Master and his Emissary,* which deals (along with much else) with the relationship between the two brain hemispheres. "If what we mean by consciousness is the part of the mind that brings the world into focus, makes it explicit, allows it to be formulated in language, and is aware of its own awareness, it is reasonable to link the conscious mind to activity almost all of which lies ultimately in the left hemisphere." (McGilchrist, 2012/2019, p.188). However, this means ignoring most of what goes on in our unconscious life, accessed via the right hemisphere. According to McGilchrist, less than 5%, and probably even less than 1%

of our life, is conscious (including the regulatory processes that run our bodies). This means that to learn more about who we are we need to extend our concept of who 'we' are to include our unconscious selves, "the experiences and states we carry with us without being aware of them". He is by no means the first to make the point that the aware self is only a part of us (among many others, Frederic Myers and William James were there first), but as a psychiatrist and neuroscientist (as well as literary scholar) he backs up this view with a wealth of evidence from the latest research in neuroscience. In his view the conscious, left hemisphere, the "emissary", builds a systematic picture of a permanent, sequential and solid world, without realising that "it is selecting from a broader world that has already been brought into being for it by the right hemisphere ... the real "master" (p. 191). According to McGilchrist, self-consciousness, "in the sense of being aware of ourselves doing something, is the left hemisphere inspecting the right" (p. 224). What we usually refer to as consciousness is selective and restricted to a small part of what we might be aware of.

Within such a framework, the concept of brain as a filter, a "reducing valve", a "modulator" that filters out of awareness anything with no direct correspondence or relevance to the bodily senses, is a possible avenue for exploring the relationship between mental reality and sensory input based in the body. Recent brain imaging research with psychedelic drugs and with other altered states of consciousness (such as hypnosis, meditation or trance) has provided support for this idea: it demonstrates that increased mental activity and performance of tasks with sophisticated mental input can be accompanied by reduced blood flow in the brain and by unexpected deactivation of the relevant neural structures (Luke, 2017). Some prodigious savants with severe neural disorders have instant access to knowledge and level of skills which, in the general population, have to be taught and learnt over a period of time (Treffert, 2010)[18]. Carl Jung talked of the "collective unconscious", Darold Treffert talks of "genetic memory", and perhaps it is relevant that in the savants the left hemisphere is often dysfunctional or damaged. None of this devalues the role of the brain as a component

---

[18] For years parents and other reliable observers reported that savants displayed extrasensory perception, but Treffert was criticised for even mentioning it in a review article in 1988. "Thus my merely reporting that there were such reports engendered censure from the scientific community" (Treffert, 2010, p. 23)

in the system of mental and physical interaction, but the evidence of parapsychology and psychical research indicates that routes by which one can access information or perform mental tasks extend beyond the familiar aspects of the brain, and into the realm of mind.

Consciousness and psi

One theory which embraces such mind phenomena has been proposed by James Carpenter in his book *First Sight: ESP and Parapsychology in Everyday Life* (Carpenter, 2012). "First sight" refers to psi, viewed not as a special ability but a universal characteristic by which information is accessed before it engages sensory perception: hence not second, but first sight. It goes on all the time without our being aware of it; consciousness begins in the unconscious. Its functioning may resemble other unconscious processes, such as subliminal perception, when our senses register something below the threshold of conscious perception. The idea that we have preconscious experiences, that we respond to stimuli without being aware of it, has been around for a long time and has been demonstrated in many experiments where people have been "primed", exposed to momentary stimuli, such as images, too quickly for them to register in consciousness, but their conscious reaction is a response to the unconscious stimulus. Carpenter sees consciousness as a continuum, where we use psi to unconsciously reach out beyond our physical boundaries for guidance on what to attend to consciously. On such a view there is nothing strange in the fact that we can produce unconscious physical reactions before becoming aware of our decisions. Benjamin Libet carried out experiments, which recorded readiness potentials (unconscious motor activity) in subjects, a fraction of a second before the conscious decision to carry out a simple task such as flexing a finger. Much has been made of the implications of these results for the question of free will but, in the words of Iain McGilchrist, "this is only a problem if one imagines that, for me to decide something, I have to have willed it with the conscious part of my mind. Perhaps my unconscious is every bit as much 'me'" (McGilchrist, 2012, p. 187).

There is no need to postulate psi in experiments such as Libet's. However, all the psi evidence (and there is plenty of it) quoted by Carpenter fits in with other evidence demonstrating that our unconscious is capable of more than we know consciously. Interestingly, Carpenter's evidence for psi blends with that for subliminal responses generally, where participants in experiments are simply responding to events (such as watching pictures that appear on the screen) while measurements are being taken of their physiological responses (such as electrodermal activity, functional magnetic resonance etc.). The difference is that in experiments demonstrating psi, there is the presentiment effect: *the physical responses by the subjects precede the events to which they are supposed to respond.* The events do not yet exist at the time when the response happens; they are still to be randomly generated by computers.

However, as has been said before, by necessity testing has its limits; by definition, testing cannot push the boundaries of a subject. It has to be limiting – you have to define your hypothesis, your procedure, and how you will judge the result. But since we do not know the boundaries of psi and how it works, the unexpected keeps happening, and examples of it abound. You have Felicia Parise, one of the successful subjects in the experiments at the Maimonides Dream Laboratory, who, instead of dreaming about the target, dreams about her granny sitting in a pool of blood – which is what actually happened to her granny – but she misses the target, so that is not a hit! (Honorton, 1993, p. 65). Matthew Manning, focus of purposeful poltergeist activity in his childhood, who later became a healer, is not much good with tests involving technology, but the equipment keeps breaking down around him (Gregory, 1982, p. 301). Such results tell you something, but not what you were testing for. Naturally, your hypotheses are based on what you know and can extrapolate from, but if you are trying to grasp the extent of the field you are meant to examine, you have to be prepared to find the unexpected, the "unknown unknown". To find out how far a field extends (within our accessible experience), it helps to observe the phenomena at their strongest, at full stretch.

Carpenter based his model only on experimental evidence, and psi elicited at unconscious level. It provides a framework for psi that is very close to the mainstream evidence for the deep connection between our unconscious and our conscious activities. That connection has been demonstrated and well established by experimental psychology and it is now generally accepted that we know more than we are aware of, and absorb information at a subliminal level. It makes good sense to start with the assumption that psi also operates continuously at a low level throughout the population, rather than being an anomaly, a special ability that only emerges in special subjects and under special conditions. We have good evidence for psi operating in this way and having to be "coaxed" into becoming conscious to become apparent, such as in experiments where people know, and can report when they are being stared at, even when isolated from the person doing the staring, or know in advance who is going to telephone them, or the special bond between mother and baby (telepathic awareness of child's needs), (Sheldrake, 1998, 2000, 2002, 2005; Sheldrake & Smart, 2003). Thus the ability to influence at a distance, to convey messages, to see a little bit into the future, seems to be a common experience of humanity, even if it is observed only occasionally and to a limited degree in everyday life. It also has obvious practical benefits, merging into "hunches" and "gut feelings", the intuitions that help us to navigate everyday life and that may arrive via the usual sensory channels at an unconscious level. There may be a lot more psi interaction going on than we are aware of; we don't notice it because it is not flagrant; for example, we may simply note in passing that some people have all the luck. Fortunately for clairvoyance research, the US military took this idea to its logical conclusion when they decided to invest in investigating remote viewing (a form of clairvoyance aimed at identifying and describing targets, often of military significance), on learning of the possibility that the USSR was training psychic spies. Going through the personnel files, they identified those lucky soldiers who "had far fewer casualties from booby traps and ambushes than average" (McMoneagle, 2006, p. 282), and selected candidates for the project from among them[19].

Remote viewing as a project arose out of awareness of the possibility of psi and hope for its application. However, we would not be investigating psi, since most of us are not even aware of using it, were it not for its spectacular manifestations by gifted psychics, or by ordinary people, in extraordinary circumstances, that go back centuries. Good evidence for this kind of psi is abundant, some of it very well documented and prevalent throughout cultures and times, and some experimental, in the sense of being conducted under controlled conditions and aimed at achieving specific goals. It involves spontaneous psi and volitional psi.

Spontaneous psi often occurs in people with no special gifts, sometimes at times of need or crisis, as if producing a sudden welling up

---

[19] Joe McMoneagle, the first remote viewer and distinguished US Army officer, now retired, recipient of the Legion of Merit award for exceptionally meritorious conduct, has been described as "the most tested and certified psychic in history" by Ed May, the programme's director (McMoneagle, 2006, p. xxiii). For more information, see entry in SPR's *Psi Encyclopedia*.

of emotional awareness of a moment of transition, usually concerning someone close. On the other hand, it can also involve trivial events; what are interesting are the patterns, which emerge from the reports of people's experiences. Louisa E. Rhine, wife of Joseph Rhine and researcher in her own right, started a collection of spontaneous cases at the Rhine Institute, by now containing thousands of accounts. That collection accepted cases without checking their veracity, on the principle that, given sufficient numbers, the possible errors would cancel each other out and not contaminate the whole. Later analyses showed that these unselected cases shared the same characteristics with the thoroughly corroborated and verified cases in the *Phantasms of the Living* collection from the nineteenth century (1886). An analysis carried out in the 1980s on cases from different times and cultures showed that the reports mainly involved people who were close to the person having the experience. In each collection the trigger seemed to be emotional concern over a serious threat to the person important to the experiencer. The form of the experience could be anything from a vague unease or sense of dread, or a dream, to seeing an apparition of the person when awake. Most such experiences relate to serious and negative events, and very few concern material damage or loss (Schouten, 1981, 1983). More recent collections seem to have a much larger proportion of dreams (traditionally a state conducive to divination), mostly precognitive, which may reflect cultural changes in an age when immediate communication is so much easier than in the days gone by. However, after-death communications (ADCs), experiences interpreted as messages from the dead, have by now acquired a literature and Internet databases of their own.

What is psi for?

While we might all be capable of spontaneous spectacular psi under some circumstances, volitional psi requires a degree of talent and skill. Instead of emotional welling up, it involves an effort to achieve a specific state of consciousness. This includes suspending sensory and intellectual input, clearing the mind to enable it to receive targeted information. That information then has to be processed into conscious content that can be communicated to others. There are techniques, such as ganzfeld, where the subjects are put into a relaxed state and sensorially isolated by having their eyes covered and listening to white noise, aimed at producing such mental states. However, while experiments have produced statistically significant results, it is still the case that people who are consistently successful, to the point of making the information obtained in this way useful, are rare, and even they are successful only some of the time. When the military project of remote viewing was established in the USA in the 1970s, attempts were made to discover what makes outstanding remote viewers special by examining their personalities, family histories, beliefs and physiology, but there was nothing obvious that linked them. What many mediums and clairvoyants do have in common is a background of some kind of trauma or damage, physical or emotional, often in childhood. Interestingly, some people who have undergone near-death experiences also develop psychic abilities afterwards, something not always welcome, especially if it takes the form of disrupting electrical/ electronic equipment. It might be argued that existence in the form of a physical body limits the mind's capacities, while acquiring greater psi powers may mean reducing the mind-body integration.

Thus it seems that attempts to find general applications for clairvoyance may be unlikely to succeed. The theory of Psi Mediated Instrumental Response (PMIR), developed by the psychologist Rex Stanford, attempts to explain psi in terms of its usefulness for survival (Duggan, 2020), as unconscious need-related behaviour guided by psi; however, it does not seem particularly effective as a survival tool. The unconscious scanning demonstrated by presentiment experiments, to which we can link the staring experiments described earlier, shows that our boundaries are fluid, but, as far as we know, no known species relies on psi for survival (Grosso, 2017, p. 18); it is too indeterminate, too undifferentiated to be relied on instead of physical senses in the physical world. In fact, it does not look as if physical life needs a high level of consciousness for survival; bacteria do very well by concentrating on basic needs without pondering the meaning of life (as far as we know). Spontaneous cases may be impressive, but are hardly reliable and, thus, dangerous in terms of evolutionary development as a survival tool, while even the best practitioners of volitional psi do not claim reliability. In fact, when so much of spontaneous evidence for psi concerns moments of death or crisis, it might be claimed that "it is as if the restraints on psi are lifted just when the practical advantage is minimized." If psi is not much use as a survival tool in biological terms, what evolutionary function might it have? The philosopher Michael Grosso suggests that "the function of psi is realized in the post-biological phase of our existence" (Grosso, 2017, pp. 20-21).

For Carlo Rovelli, a famous physicist, fear of death is an evolutionary error caused by our awareness of time and our being held together by memories; it is "the produce of bad automatic connection in our brain rather than something that has any use or meaning" (Rovelli, 2018, p. 177). But while Rovelli regards fear of death as an error, for Grosso it comes from the inability of the materialistic worldview to deal with the knowledge of the finiteness of life. If psi is real, it might offer a means of escaping the constraints of physical existence, of space and time. It could be adapted for survival in a wider, non-biological, or not-only-biological environment, one that transcends the physical environment; on the other hand, all-pervasive psi in the physical world would result in chaos.

The hope/expectation of "escaping the constraints of the physical" (Grosso, 2017, p. 18), of something beyond physical life, seems to be an immanent part of the human psyche. Religions in their various guises offer different options, often focused on the consequences of actions in embodied life (heaven, hell, karma). In non-religious terms there are now ideas of downloading consciousness into more resilient substrates, creating avatars or "hypercorporeal simulacra". The disjointed glimpses of psi we get at the physical level may well point to another level of complexity, a nested holarchy of processes extended in time.

Intention and its sources

One feature of psi on which many researchers and practitioners have commented is that it is usually teleological, goal oriented, and remarkably not restricted by the complexity of the task. Whether we are talking about psychic healers, ardent prayer or a person sitting in front of a random number generator trying to skew the way the numbers go, the thing they all have in common is intention, an interaction with a larger reality. When it comes to volitional clairvoyance, it is the intention that seems to be the driving force in identifying the target. According to Joe McMoneagle, one of the most famous clairvoyants today, when remote viewers discriminate among the separate targets in an area that is dense with possible landmarks, it is "almost as if they are guided to the target through instinct – or perhaps it is only through *intent*" (McMoneagle, 2013, loc. 2082). He regards it as the glue that holds everything together. Mediums with a proven track record of clairvoyance seem to be certain that, when they try to contact the deceased on behalf of the living, it is the discarnates whose intention drives the process – which is why sometimes the person who "comes through" in a sitting is not the one who was expected. Whatever the full story, intention and attention seem to be deeply involved. But where do the intending and attending come from?

Intention is a concept that seems tied to an entity that can intend, i.e., make use of information. Examining the physical substrate of information, such as the brain, has led to the model of the brain as a blueprint of circuits. Research has shown that our brain "hosts a detailed blueprint" of circuits, a "hierarchy of nested models" programmed with expectations about the outside world acquired by association and habituation in the course of evolution. For example, contrary to earlier theories, babies (and some animals!) are amazed by magic tricks, such as when an object seems to vanish; they have an intuitive grasp of various basic concepts such as space, numbers, physics and language (Deheane, 2020). Each species interprets the world on the basis of the information supplied by the senses and the models it has evolved, so it is hardly surprising that we do the same. You do not have to go beyond mainstream science to fit information into a model of evolution which allows organisms to be involved in their own development, profit from past experience, guide their own mutations and follow an upward learning curve (Davies, 2019). There is what has been described as the "automatic realm, the autopilot mode of the embodied mind, wherein prior experiences, feelings, and choices all play out in the form of conditioned habits" (Kauffman-Peil, 2015, p.15). However, this does not seem quite an adequate framework for the kind of self-examining consciousness that seeks meaning and purpose, and it definitely needs expanding if you accept the evidence of psi.

One approach to solving this problem is to regards mind/ consciousness as universal and primary. The mind is then the source of everything, and all that exists does so in the one mind. This chimes in with the increasingly popular ancient Eastern philosophies and does have the benefit of not postulating any additional forms of existence. With one universal consciousness, all physical reality that we experience – spacetime, matter and fields – is the product of the one mind. In this sense it is a "match" for materialism, but is a great deal better than materialism at coping with experiential phenomena. One can fit into it a number of non-materialistic concepts, from a continuous flow of consciousness, through cosmic reservoir of memories, Akashic records formed on a higher plane, to Sheldrake's morphogenetic fields. It may well be the case that there is a "consciousness field", or indeed more than one, underlying or penetrating the physical fields. However, such a mind-at-large is not specific enough to apply to the evidence for psi to be discussed here.[20] When it comes specifically to clairvoyance, what we find are very specific acts of intention or attention, and that entails the existence of an intender. Just as psychological processes cannot be reduced to lower-level physical processes, so these intenders cannot be summed up in a generic mind-at-large without being individualised in some way. We accept that as living beings we have a personality (or personalities), emotions, memories, intentions, and a sense of dynamic connectedness, of being one with the persons we were yesterday or 10 years ago. In other words there is a continuity of consciousness, a self that has subjective experiences; it is the "experiencer". Paul Davies in his *The Demon in the Machine* defines the self as "a slowly evolving complex pattern of stored information that can be accessed at later times and provide an information template against which fresh perceptions can be matched" (Davies, 2019, p. 195); in biology we find the pragmatic operational definition of "informational individuals", described as "aggregates that propagate information from the past to the future and have temporal integrity", thus capturing "the idea that there is something persistent about individuals", while individuality can emerge at any level of organisation; it is a process rather than an object, continuous rather than binary (Krakauer at al., 2020)[21].

We do need such a concept of self as an "informational individual" in a framework for the functioning of psi, but one that extends beyond the physical components, and beyond the information ingrained in us as a species. Our memories are malleable, can be suppressed, distorted and simply forgotten, yet we have this sense of dynamic connectedness, of recognition, between various versions of ourselves over time, and we apply this sense when we identify others even when physically they may have changed beyond recognition. There may well be a cosmic mind or a

---

[20] Here we are concerned with evidence for clairvoyance and telepathy, i.e., forms of communication; experience of transcendence at one end, or "jotts", where objects seem to slip through the fabric of reality, at the other, presumably requires a much larger worldview.

[21] It seems that as soon as we move from abstraction to specific subjects, time is assumed to be fundamental to creation.

sea of consciousness, but much of the evidence for psi points to a level of individual consciousness (or groups of consciousnesses) with capability for recognition and intention, and with a structure that makes it possible for the physical and the non-physical, biology and consciousness, to interact in ways and through mechanisms which are a mystery at our present state of knowledge. Spectacular clairvoyance, such as demonstrated by remote viewers and clairvoyants such as Krzysztof Jackowski in his psychic detection, involves catching glimpses of the past and the future, locating distant objects and persons, delving into others' emotions and motives; the more humdrum kind of clairvoyance demonstrated in, for example, the presentiment experimentation, seems to be part of our everyday lives. On the basis of this kind of evidence, Stephen Braude suggests that sensory, embodied perception should be viewed as a "special case", an aspect of a wider form of awareness (Braude, 2020, p. 212). The idea has been around for some time; H.H. Price was one of a number of philosophers to describe normal sense-perception "not as 'normal', but rather as a sub-normal and biologically-explicable limitation imposed upon an inherent and aboriginal omniscience" (Price, 1943), while the mathematician G.N.M. Tyrrell pointed out that the so-called 'normal' perception only seems so because it is a given, not subjected to philosophical analysis (Tyrrell, 1935).

Clairvoyance as a fundamental form of awareness: the implications

Adopting the view that embodied perception is a special case of a more general form of awareness, one that is constrained by the organism's physical limitations, allows us to integrate the various strands of evidence that on other views do not seem to fit together. One area where the evidence is abundant, persistent and comes from both real-life and experiments, is clairvoyance and telepathy. However, even those who accept the evidence do not usually start with the assumption adopted here, that clairvoyance is the basic way "in which at least some complex organisms acquire information about mental and physical states of the world" (Braude, 2020, p. 212). Yet it is a logical consequence of the view that consciousness – and therefore information and communication – is in some way fundamental to living systems.

Carpenter's experiments point to the conclusion that psi operates all the time at an unconscious level. However, in everyday physical life it only becomes observable when it takes a spectacular form, either in spontaneous cases or volitionally in gifted individuals. Clairvoyance and telepathy (both restricted to the living) and mediumship (understood as obtaining information from discarnate sources) are sometimes used as arguments for and against the possibility of survival of bodily death in philosophical debates in parapsychology. However, what all these kinds of experiences have in common is that at times they demonstrate, beyond reasonable doubt, that personal consciousness can function purposefully outside and beyond the body. When trying to make sense of things that are impossible but happen anyway, it is useful to view them as a spectrum without defining its limits, and without postulating specific frameworks for such functioning[22]. The first task is to learn as much as possible about the kind of information being obtained/ transferred, the nature and characteristics of the recipients and the possible sources of the information, even though the mechanisms that link them elude explanation.

We use the term "clairvoyance", since it is well established and immediately understood (ESP is a wider, umbrella term for a variety of extrasensory perceptions), but perhaps Elizabeth Mayer's "extraordinary knowing" (Mayer, 2008) might be a more fitting description for the kind of awareness that can involve intention (causal powers, including physical influence), perspectival views impossible through ordinary senses (such as identifying a specific card in a deck of cards)[23], locating objects in distant places, and looking into the future as well as the past (precognition and retrocognition). Recently, clairvoyance has also been described as non-local consciousness. However you describe it, the effects are impossible to achieve with our ordinary physical senses, while psychics themselves employ a variety of methods in achieving their aims, and offer different interpretations of what happens when they reach out to the target. Sometimes the descriptions of the experience imply being out of the body and transporting oneself elsewhere; in a sense that is obviously true, since the body of the experiencer is at one specific location and the target at another (including another mind).

---

[22] Such as a substrate that would "house" a discarnate information pattern, e.g., an "astral body".

[23] " ... some evidence of clairvoyance can be taken to show that veridical awareness of physical states of affairs is possible even when there's no actual point of view from which the states of affairs can be accessed by sensory means" (Braude, 2020, p. 206)

OBE states (out-of-body experience, where sometimes one sees one's stationary body and moves away from it), bilocation (the physical body being in one place but the person being seen somewhere else), trance or other altered states of consciousness also form part of the psychics' experience. The complexity of this experience has aptly been described as a "cognitive stew" for reasons that have been familiar to psychical research for a long time. It has also been accepted for a long time that clairvoyance has to be at least a two-stage process, with the initial impressions gained in a manner still unknown, which then have to make their way through the conscious processing in a variety of forms, often as symbols or images idiosyncratic to the person, in most cases with accurate information mixed up with irrelevancies (Braude, 1994). Much of psychical research has been devoted to trying to disentangle and identify the components of this "stew".

4

A BRIEF HISTORY OF CLAIRVOYANCE RESEARCH

~

The beginnings

It could be claimed with some justification that it was Franz Anton Mesmer's (1734-1815) discovery of "animal magnetism", of people exerting a mysterious influence on each other, that gave rise to the development both of psychology and psychical research. Originally a healing treatment, thought to work through a "magnetic fluid" that passed between the healer and the healee, it came to be associated with altered states of consciousness such as trance and somnambulism, with evidence of paranormal cognition, and the phenomenon became widespread and popular. Andrew Jackson Davis (1826–1910), one of the founders of Spiritualism, started out as an itinerant somnambulist and dictated his works in a magnetic trance. This was part of the rise of Spiritualism, and news of it spread throughout the United States and Europe.

It also spurred scientific investigations of unconscious mental life and various states of consciousness, such as those produced by hypnosis and suggestion. In the 1870s and 1880s a number of distinguished scientists, among them Charles Richet, Jean-Martin Charcot and Pierre Janet, explored these experiences, developing a variety of approaches and schools of thought, while research into hypnotism led to it being used for anaesthesia (Crabtree, 1988). Some of the founders of the SPR, such as Frederic Myers and Henry Sidgwick, also collaborated in this work, which clearly had implications for psychical research. Myers's seminal *Human Personality and Its Survival of Bodily Death* (1903) both benefitted from and contributed to this research into the subconscious. The work of these researchers also contributed to the establishment of psychology as a distinct branch of learning; previously, during the 1870s and 1880s, psychology was often regarded as a hobby for philosophers and doctors.

From the earliest, paranormal phenomena were associated with magnetism, "and for upwards of fifty years, remained a central feature of the animal magnetic scene" (Gauld, 1995, p. 62). They continued as part of the scene as research progressed into the various anomalous states of mind exhibited by somnambulists and a variety of mental disorders. The fascinating early accounts of experiments in hypnosis, suggestion and the resulting clairvoyance are unfortunately marred by "an almost complete failure to appreciate the powerful workings of 'experimenter effect' and 'doctrinal compliance' upon mesmerized or hypnotized subjects, and to grasp the methods of controlled experimentation which are necessary to offset these dangers" (Gauld, 1995, pp. 266-7), although some researchers did recognise these problems.

As has already been said, the body originally leading that research was the Society for Psychical Research, established in 1882, but soon it was joined in its efforts by the American Society for Psychical Research, and during the early 20th century many societies with the same aim sprung up throughout Europe. Much of the clairvoyance research briefly described below stems from the efforts in the English-speaking areas, but the other less well-known examples also highlight the same patterns that emerge from different kinds of experimental and other evidence.

Judging the quality of evidence in any context involves a number of aspects. You need to assess any reporting in terms of how well it is documented (both in experiments and field research); how verifiable it is; how credible and trustworthy the researchers or witnesses are; what other interpretations might be possible; and whether there are sufficient numbers of consistent reports/experiments to form discernible patterns. When it comes to clairvoyance, good evidence is abundant enough to make selection of examples quite difficult.

Alexis Didier: early and well-documented clairvoyance

Formal research into telepathy and clairvoyance started to develop towards the end of the nineteenth century, but anecdotal reports of such events go back centuries. However, some anecdotal reports are documented in a way that meets the criterion of evidentiality, with extensive contemporary literature. One such case is that of the French clairvoyant Alexis Didier (1826-1886). He was able to identify concealed targets and recount their histories, discern a specified phrase in a book, describe strangers' lives and houses in accurate detail, "go" to places he had never visited, or locate missing people and objects, very much as the best remote viewers do today. Alexis and his brother made a living out of public performances of clairvoyance, which tends to give rise to suspicion, but the famous then contemporary conjurer, J.R. Robert-Houdin, tested Alexis to his satisfaction, and many experiments simply preclude cheating unless one postulates collusion among a number of otherwise reliable witnesses who were strangers to each other (Beloff, 1993, pp. 28-33).

One incident, reported in the respectable journal *The Zoist* in 1845, had two confirming accounts, with Didier describing the contents of a case unknown to anyone apart from the owner, whom he had not met before. It was a bone sawn off the leg of the case's owner after a war injury; Didier not only described the leg, a very offbeat object by any measure, but also where and how the injury occurred, and the circumstances of the event (Gauld, 1995, pp. 236-238).

Didier's clairvoyance fits in with the results from later research in terms of what aids performance and how psi works: he needed to be put into a special state (hypnosis) to perform; he found it helpful to have a personal possession to "guide" him to the right person or place (psychometry); and he provided a great deal of additional information about the situation. However, in these early reports, there is no attempt to differentiate between telepathy (which could have operated in the case above) and clairvoyance. In fact, the seminal *Phantasms of the Living* (1886) assumed telepathy as the theoretical framework to account for the phenomena.

Telepathy or clairvoyance – early experiments

Many early experiments conducted by the SPR (carried out alongside collecting spontaneous accounts), some dating back to the 1880s, were aimed at investigating telepathy, referred to as thought reading, thought transference, or mind-to-mind communication. Some used playing cards as targets; some were conducted at home as a parlour game. One of the most successful and thoroughly reported later series involved Professor Gilbert Murray (1866-1957), a classical scholar and well-known intellectual, and a variety of friends. Murray would be sent out of the room, and one of those present, the agent, would choose a subject to be identified by Murray on his return[24]. To give a simple example: the agent thinks of the *Lusitania*, and on his return Murray says "...an awful impression of naval disaster. I should think it was the torpedoing of the *Lusitania*" (Koestler, 1972 p. 36). In his SPR Presidential Address in 1916, Gilbert Murray, speaking from experience suggested that telepathy was operating everywhere. This was already pointing in the direction of the theory proposed by Carpenter discussed earlier: that we use our psi, our "first sight", all the time without being aware of it.

Many experiments supported this suggestion, and showed that, while thought transference was going on, what was transmitted was not just the intended images. An account, which resonated well with the public, was published in a book called *Mental Radio* in 1930, by the well-known writer Upton Sinclair. His wife, Mary Craig, tried, among other things, to reproduce drawings made by her brother-in-law in another city at an appointed time. Many were successful, but of particular interest were those where she "got" more than the drawing, or images from the sender's mind instead of the drawing: on one occasion the sender drew a chair, but since at some point he was looking at the chair through the vertical bars at the end of his bed these were reproduced as well. On another occasion she got none of the drawings prepared by her husband, but drew the strange moon that he was looking at and called for her to come out and see shortly after she had drawn its image[25]. One of many instances of telepathy going awry was an experiment in telepathy between two remarkable

---

[24] Auditory hyperacuity was considered as an explanation, but there were many cases where it could not apply.

[25] What added credibility to these reports was a preface to the book by Albert Einstein (written for the German edition), the author's close friend.

sensitives, Eileen Garrett (founder of the Parapsychology Foundation) and Rosalind Heywood (author and member of the SPR). There, instead of the object that Rosalind had put in the appointed place (a photograph of her favourite philosopher) as the target, at the appointed time Eileen got the figure of the Divine Mother. Not only was this unexpected, it also seemed to follow Rosalind's train of thought: at the time she was dwelling on the image involved in her peak experience in an experiment with mescaline (Heywood 1971, pp. 56-7).

Telepathy and clairvoyance experiments were conducted at the Institut Métapsychique International (IMI) in France from the early 1900s by such investigators as Rene Warcollier, a renowned chemical engineer and one of the Institute's founders; Eugene Osty, a medical doctor; and Charles Richet, Nobel-prize winning physiologist (Osty, 1923). It was observed that perceptions were received in fragments, and, as with Mary Sinclair, sketching appeared to be more helpful than descriptions, since the content was likely to be misperceived at the conscious, verbal level. As we are now well aware, premature attempts at interpretation (analytical overlay) can distort the basic information obtained unconsciously.

There were also experiments in group telepathy, such as those carried out on the initiative of Dr Angelos Tanagras, President of the Athenian Society for Psychical Research, between his team in Athens and groups in Paris, Berlin, Vienna, London, Rome and Warsaw during the 1920s and 30s. A series of experiments in these different cities had two groups of participants, gathering at the same time and alternately sending images to each other (Palikari, 2020). With similar procedures, they achieved similar results, and the account, below, is based on the reports of the experiments between Athens and Warsaw. These reports are both quantitative and qualitative, showing reproduced images as well as discussing achievements of individuals within the Polish group.

In the series of experiments between Athens and Warsaw between October 1928 and June 1929, one group would concentrate its attention on a particular drawing (large enough to be visible to about a dozen people), and the other group would try to reproduce that drawing; after two experiments the groups would exchange roles; the "sender" group" would try to "receive" and the "receiving" group would try to "send". Only the group leaders, Prosper Szmurło and Angelos Tanagras, knew each other briefly, but the experiments produced a number of remarkable hits. Since Tanagras had a team of mediums while some on the Polish team were known psychics (but not professional) as well, this is not surprising.

There was a variety of target images: tools, objects, body parts, plants and animals, music notes, numbers etc. The experimenters were aware that using a limited set of targets (e.g. letters) would make it easier to calculate probability, but they chose not to. The images transmitted came through in a variety of forms and sensory channels: visually or conceptually (e.g., the target was a key but one participant drew a keyhole); represented as a fragment of an image, sometimes supplemented with extra material, or seen from a different angle. The assessment of the work of the Greek-Polish collaboration was based on numbers of shared features, and the results were divided into five categories presented in tabular form, from "total identity" (perfect reproduction), to cases of association; however, even the disqualified drawings had some connection with the target. All the drawings by every receiver were compared not only to the particular session but also to those produced at all the other sessions. Percentages of "hits" varied significantly among participants (allowing for the numbers of experiments attended and drawings produced), with some producing a very high number. Among other things, they tried transmitting whole scenes and events narrated to the group, but this produced too many images that might all somehow be relevant to the target (Rzewuski, 1929; Szmurło, 1929).

Some unexpected by-products were also observed: sometimes the drawing being transmitted was sensed and drawn, not during transmission, but during the next experiment (the well known displacement effect observed in card-guessing experiments); there was also influence of telepathy within the same group rather than clairvoyantly identifying the target, while the Athenian "misses" were sometimes very similar to those produced in Warsaw.

Fig. 1. Selection of drawings [Rysunki] from the Athens-Warsaw section
of the experiment. Column headings: 1. Sent from Athens;
2. Drawn simultaneously in Warsaw.
Names of participants are given under the drawings.

The results of the telepathy experiments reported in *Mental Radio*, as
well as the drawings produced by the teams in Warsaw and in Athens,
bear great similarity to those produced by Uri Geller under shielded
conditions and described in *Mind Reach* (Targ & Puthoff, 2005). Even so,
this impressive-looking and consistent body of evidence from different
times does not by itself take us much further in understanding the
processes involved. However, over the years, particularly during the

1930s and 40s, much progress was made in experimental procedures, eliminating the possibility of fraud and leakage of information by increasingly ingenious use of technology and more sophisticated statistical techniques. Card guessing experiments going back to the early twentieth century were subjected to statistical reviews, while later experiments aimed to avoid pitfalls by using such techniques as lists of randomized targets (subjects for drawings were chosen using random tables to find words in dictionaries), weighting the hits to avoid stereotypes (the less popular the item the higher the value), isolating the experimenter from the participants, and having independent judges (Carrington, 1941). Large-scale testing with limited targets, such as the experiments with the Zener cards used by Rhine and his team, provided statistical evidence for psi but also showed the questionability of the assumption that the impressions came from the mind of the agent, the "sender", and not from the target itself being directly accessed by the percipient (as, for example, where the agent guesses correctly the next target before it has been selected by the sender).

Clearly, mind-to-mind transference did (and does) happen, and increasingly efforts were made to eliminate unintended transference of mind content. In fact, the problem of disentangling the possibility of telepathy from clairvoyance, and telepathy and clairvoyance among the living from messages from the dead is still an important issue in psychical research.

Remote viewing as "best practice" clairvoyance: development and procedures

The success rate in the reports of earlier researchers is impossible to estimate because there is no common framework for assessing it. However, the arrival of the technique of remote viewing, a disciplined form of clairvoyance/psychic detection, has been very useful in clarifying some of the issues involved.

From the 1970s to 1995, research into psi was of interest to US government agencies and the military. This interest originated with reports of psi research in the USSR, and the concern over the possible threat of psychic influence/infiltration by foreign powers. The research started out at the Stanford Research Institute with two physicists, Harold Puthoff and Russell Targ (Targ & Puthoff, 1977/2005), and continued with less publicity over many years under the direction of another eminent physicist, Ed May, from late 1975 through 1995 (May, 2014). Much has been written about the programme, and the final official report was negative. However, that report was based on a sliver of data and reflected neither the programme's true achievements nor its shortcomings. The controversy still goes on, and none of the arguments are relevant in the discussion of the characteristics of remote viewing itself, but it is helpful to bear in mind the judgment by statistician Jessica Utts[26] in her report to the CIA in 1995: "Using the standards applied to any other areas of science, it is concluded that psychic functioning has been well established. The statistical results of the studies examined are far beyond what is expected by chance." In fact, according to her, the data is stronger than the experimental evidence showing that aspirin prevents heart attacks (Targ, 2012, pp. 44-45).

The name "remote viewing" was chosen for the project as more neutral than clairvoyance in terms of popular associations, but the project was also distinguished by the procedures it adopted. Joe McMoneagle, probably the best-known star performer of the remote viewing programme, offers the following description of the process:

> remote viewing is the ability to produce information that is correct about a place, event, person, object or concept which is located somewhere else in time and space, and which is completely blind to the remote viewer and others taking part in the process of collecting the information.

What makes it a special kind of clairvoyance is that the experiments follow well-defined protocols, the purpose of which is to "bring some validity and credibility to the study of paranormal functioning ..." (McMoneagle, 2000, pp. 22-23).

Among the earliest remote viewers used in Targ and Puthoff's experiments in the early 1970s were Ingo Swann, a well-known psychic and artist, and Pat Price, a former policeman. In the early experiments the remote viewer would describe his/her impressions of the target scene to one researcher, while the other set out for the target, learning its location only after having left the premises, by opening one of the sealed

---

[26] Jessica Utts is Professor Emerita at the Department of Statistics, University of California. Fellow of the American Statistical Association and the Institute of Mathematical Statistics, she served as the 111th president of the American Statistical Association in 2016.

envelopes containing possible targets. There were spectacular successes, which led to later experiments where the "blinding" reached the point of the target being identified only by its geographical coordinates (Ingo Swann's idea) – yet this did not affect the quality of the results (Targ, 2012, p. 25). Even when the viewers were provided with coordinates encrypted into an indecipherable code the results did not deteriorate (Gruber, 1999, pp. 64-5), as if intention alone was sufficient for clairvoyance to work, an impressive level of sophistication in experimental clairvoyance.

The project also included the development of a statistical method of judging success known as rank order judging. After a remote viewing session an independent judge would be shown the viewer's response and the actual target among other potential targets (chosen from a pool of images, usually five), and rank them according to the "best fit" to the viewer's response (Targ & Puthoff, 2005). This method was adopted since it was the only way of defining "chance", an essential aspect of statistical analysis: If chance alone is at work, what is the probability that a *target* would be chosen that matches this *response* as well as or better than does the actual target?' ... In order to accomplish this purpose, a properly conducted experiment uses a set of targets defined in advance. The target for each remote viewing is then selected randomly, in such a way that the probability of getting each possible target is known". (Schwartz, 2014, p. 5)

Today the procedure is more likely to be computerised, and the procedures for matching the target image with the viewer's mentation by independent judges are also being continually refined. A variety of methodologies and applications has grown around the process – such as Controlled Remote Viewing (CRV), Technical Remote Viewing, Scientific Remote Viewing, Associative Remote Viewing (the last one aimed at forecasting market movements) – all with slightly different procedures. However, they all rely on sessions that are properly recorded, reported and analysed.

The judging procedure in experiments, while amenable to statistical analysis, is not without drawbacks. While constantly being refined, it still suffers from reducing qualitative data to hits and misses, does not allow for displacement (where the participant might give an accurate description of a decoy target), while judges may put different interpretations on possible correspondences where, for example, sketches may be detailed or simplistic (Katz et al., 2021).

Whatever the later developments in remote viewing, these experiments helped to establish the protocols used later by the CIA and the military projects in real life, and their protocols helped to demonstrate how clairvoyance worked and what helped to achieve it. Both the experiments and real-life tasks in remote viewing rely on meticulous record keeping and independent assessment of the information provided by the psychic, something often lacking in verifiable (because they achieved the result) but unstructured reports of spectacular feats of clairvoyance. In real-life tasks the missions were generally handed to the remote viewers only after all other ways of gathering intelligence proved insufficient, very much as in cases of police turning to psychic detection when no other clues are available. The rate of success of 60% – 65% in a session of this kind would be regarded as remarkable, a necessary reality check in an area where there is a spectrum of misconceptions about what is and what is not possible (McMoneagle, 2000, pp. 27-33). However, when the objective is to identify a real-life situation, matching the information provided by the viewers with the target takes place within a different framework, and what counts is its usefulness. There also might be many sessions by a number of remote viewers revisiting the target before coming up with a report. Remarkably, they tend to get much convergent, accurate information.

Some important findings in clairvoyance/remote viewing research

The significance of time

Remote viewing experiments showed early on that it was also important to specify the point in time when the target is to be viewed, since clairvoyance was not limited to the present, but could range over the past and the future to an unknown extent. This feature (retrocognition and precognition) was also recognised in earlier experiments, with, for example, Eugene Osty asking his mediums to keep going back or forward in time to find the right person among those who handled the psychometric object (Barrington, 2019, p.102); also, displacement in card experiments became a well-known feature. Lack of awareness of the need to specify the period could lead to confusion: Pat Price, a gifted psychic, an ex-policeman and early subject of remote viewing experimentation, identified a water plant instead of a swimming pool complex – but he saw the target as it had been 60 years previously. On another occasion, he described the target half an hour before the viewer reached it, demonstrating both precognition and the superfluity of a viewer (Targ, 2012, p. 61, 63).

Different psychics, different talents

Remote viewing research has also thrown new light on the characteristics of the kind of people involved and the kind of training that would lead to success. It turned out that selected individuals (six in the case of the Star Gate project) were much better at the tasks than unselected subjects, while mass screening showed that only about 1% of volunteers were consistently successful. Training or practice did not make a perceptible difference; neither did distance between the target and the subject, nor electromagnetic shielding. On the other hand, precognitive remote viewing with selected participants, with the target chosen *after* the session, also produced successful results (Utts, in Gruber, 1999, p. 91).

Remote viewing experiments also revealed that the viewers had preferences – things that some excelled at: "each person tended to focus on certain aspects of the remote target complex and to exclude others, so that each had an individual pattern of response, like a signature". For Swann, it was maps and topographical features; for Price, sensory experiences (Targ & Puthoff, 2005). Later viewers demonstrated a similar pattern, with one being especially good at "personal matters", another at artistic drawings and yet another at precise focusing on targets, while Joe McMoneagle produced "astonishingly accurate sketches of technical objects" (Gruber, 1999, p.70). This, again, echoes Osty's claim for the need to adapt to the individual psychics: "Study of this faculty of hyper-cognition soon reveals that those who possess it differ so much in their individual powers that no two are alike ... each seizes on some fragmentary part of the whole reality, the part cognised being variable in its nature and extent ... One person may be a dowser and nothing more. Another having remarkable powers of perception of human personalities, and for whom other lives have no secrets, can grasp no other reality. Mme Przybylska,[27] endowed with a semi-divine faculty of perceiving the future, is perhaps incapable of saying what is happening in the next room, or of finding a bit of copper buried in the ground" (Osty, 1923, pp. 44-45). Experimental procedures do not, on the whole, take this entanglement of ability and personality into account, and it awaits more systematic investigation.

---

[27] Maria Przybylska (Lebiedziński, 1928) was Vice President of the Polish Society for Psychical Research, as well as a clairvoyant famous for her ability to see current and future events in a literal form, as if she was their witness.

Targets: what kinds and how to reach them

In a properly conducted remote viewing session nobody present knows what the target is, while the target is real, well defined and verifiable, even though it can be mental, such as thoughts, words or feelings (McMoneagle, 2000, pp. 27-33). In various experiments, carried out by different researchers, the tasks were very varied, and included describing geographical locations at coordinates, sealed envelopes, small targets in boxes and even microdots. In case the process involved signal transmission (the hypothesis usually adopted in the research in Soviet Union), the viewers were placed in a variety of environments and shielded in a variety of ways, such as the Faraday cage and even in a submarine. A review of this research by Caroline Watt at the University of Edinburgh concluded that the most perceivable targets were emotionally significant or dramatic (Schwartz, 2014, p. 12), pointing towards a rationale for the predominance of such features in spontaneous cases.

Precognition: non-existent targets

One of the most important aspects of much of the continuing experimentation, including various forms of remote viewing, is that at the time of the viewing the target has not yet been selected. This is the same effect as in the presentiment experiments discussed by Carpenter in his *First sight*, but on a larger scale. And in associative remote viewing, precognition is not incidental but the consciously intended outcome on the basis of which commercial decisions are taken (playing the stock market). In the words of Paul Smith, a successful ex-military remote viewer himself, "the present event A is the perceiving, sketching, and describing of the target to be observed in the future. The future event B is the showing of the object to the viewer hours or days hence. In either case, it is clear the present is being influenced by a conscious, intentional act to unfold in a certain way, and nothing is being changed from some way it had already become".[28]

In his doctoral dissertation on physicalism, Smith puts forward a view of precognition that seems both simple and persuasive. According to

---

[28] This is part of Smith's response to the hypothesis of retrocausation, postulated as the explanation for small-scale results, such as affecting runs of numbers on REGs (the original results being affected by later examination). However, it clearly will not do for large-scale events (much as we might like to change misfortunes of the past, thinking "if only ... "), or any other psi occurrences.

Smith, that debate concerns *causal* order: in the physical world, causes cannot come before events. He describes precognition as "a person in the present 'reaching forward' to bring back information that affects an event or events now, as the present unfolds". It is the information about the possible developments that can be acted upon, very much as in his everyday-life example: "The thrown ball would have broken the window if William had not jumped up and caught it in his baseball mitt." The original causal chain has been replaced by another causal chain (William catches the ball, the window is not broken) (Smith, 2009, pp. 260-263). In experiments, the information "brought back" when the target is compared to the viewer's description tends to be assessed in statistical terms; in some spontaneous cases the knowledge "brought back" can be sudden and spectacular[29]. But the only loop is informational, in the way that general information is causal in informing decision-making for action. Thus there is nothing inconsistent about precognition of future events influencing the present: so far, so simple. However, we have no way of accounting for how it might happen in terms of current physics, and the evidence for precognition should not exist. Precognition experiments show the causal chain's starting and ending points, but not the links between them. Thus the data is evidence for what Smith describes as "intermittently truncated causal chains", which violate our assumptions about causation. As he puts it, "If human perceptions were not restricted to the confines of the time-space continuum, then it would be a (conceptually) simple matter to "pop out" of the present and "pop in" to the future to access the future event, much as in the case of migrating salmon, where water flows from *upstream* to *downstream* around a dam through a fish ladder, allowing the salmon on their way to spawn to get around the dam by taking the fish-ladder detour *upstream*, avoiding the otherwise insurmountable obstacle". The problem is that human perception *is* restricted, so one ends up postulating a "truly non-physical aspect of the universe" (Smith, 2009, pp. 266-274).

---

[29] An account by Emil Zmenak tells of his wife having the impression of getting a call from the police and "seeing" a body without legs (she is concerned and does not want her husband to go out). Later that evening there is a car accident in which a man's body is trapped in a car with his legs broken, and the police call Zmenak's wife to let her know that her husband is delayed because he is a witness. The incident is confirmed by judicial records, and reported in *New Horizons*, Journal of the *New Horizons* Research Foundation produced by A.R.G. Owen and his wife Iris 1972-1978 (Zmenak, 1972).

Remote viewing experiments aimed specifically at precognition may be the most important evidence for psi, and clairvoyance in particular. They are small-scale, numerous, statistically significant, use scientific methodology, and produce inexplicable results.

In experimental evidence the targets may be ordinary cards, Zener cards, sealed envelopes, or objects concealed in containers. They seem simple until one remembers that there is no physical position in space from which they could be observed (excluding the "usual suspects" of incorrect procedures), while targets that do not exist at the time of the test, are still to be generated, defy our ideas about temporal flow.

In real life, the targets are not so precisely defined, they are more "diffuse", involving people and events to be located and described. They are not so "pristine" as experimental ones, but the objective is different in real life: it is to get a result by linking to the target by whatever means are available.

Psychometry

Over the years, various such ways of linking to the target have been established, including psychometry. In psychometry the psychic handles an object associated with the target person, place or object. Much research in this area was carried out in France in the first half of the 20th century, using a number of "metagnomes", and a variety of psychometric objects, the most successful being those which had been in close contact with the person being sought, as well as photos or letters. Among the famous cases there is one where Osty describes a psychometrist being given a "neckwrapper" belonging to a missing 82-year-old man who did not return from his walk on a large estate. The psychometrist knew immediately that the man was dead; she retraced the man's steps and eventually by the third sitting, pinpointed the location of the body in spite of the confusingly similar landmarks such as trees and water (Osty 1923, pp. 105-9). During the same period Gustav Pagenstecher was conducting experiments with just one psychometrist, Senora Z (Zierold), who (to take one incident) made 35 correct statements out of 38 regarding an old letter she was given to hold, concerning the author of the letter (Beloff, 1993, p. 98). When asked to describe the fate of a person or an object, Stefan Ossowiecki asked to hold or touch something personal, including photographs.

Psychometry is still very much a feature in modern psychic detection, and the idea of being able to glimpse the history of the psychometric object turns up in the accounts of many later psychic virtuosi. In the 1970s, the well-known researcher Charles Honorton encouraged a gifted psychic Felicia Parise to "exercise her 'psychic muscles' in a variety of informal ways, such as trying to pick up information about people by free associating about personal belongings, such as a ring or a watch, something at which she became successful (Honorton, 1993, p.66). According to Osty, in most cases it is most unlikely that the object carries some kind of "imprint": "The function of the object put into the hands of the percipient is not to furnish direct information. It seems rather a means, provisionally necessary to some and not to others, to enable them to link themselves to the real source of information" (Osty, 1923, p. 175). We are still far from identifying what the real source of information might be.

On the whole, the data from the less formal (and usually earlier) reports tends to be a lot richer than that from experimental ones. Much of the early research into remote viewing started with the question "Is this real?"

Stephan Schwartz started from the perspective of his in-depth study of reports of Edgar Cayce's sessions that left him in no doubt of the reality of clairvoyance. Edgar Cayce (1878-1945), a famous psychic, left thousands of extremely well documented and verified reports of his readings, many of them done by correspondence, amounting to high quality "double-blind outbound remote viewings". Schwartz makes the point that "spiritual experiences and nonlocal consciousness experiences are the same thing in different contexts, using different language", and gives examples of Cayce's sensory engagement with the target: "He's not here yet ... he's still on a bus ... a wonderful smell of flowers ..." (Cayce's statement), with the feedback report: "At the time the Reading was scheduled he was stuck on the bus... "We had just opened his window and the smell of Jasmine filled the room.", or "Yes we have the body ... quite a lot of body ... Lovely pajamas ..." (Cayce's statement) and the feedback: "She is quite overweight, although how Cayce knew that I can not guess ... She had on her new pajamas, with which she was very pleased" (Schwartz, 2014, pp. 22-23). Since Cayce presumably handled the letters, or at least had them to hand, psychometry may have played a part in the richness of his responses. Perhaps we might learn something about the relationship between the nature of the target and the kind of information obtained from it by systematically comparing what "comes through" in real-life reports, earlier experiments, and reports that predate the formal remote viewing sessions and do not exclude human involvement from target creation; this is something that still remains to be done.

Different times, different psychics, similar experience

Having gone through the literature produced over many decades, in an article written in 1964, the researcher Rhea White quotes many authors who describe the same stages of volitional clairvoyance, even though they use a variety of words:

1. Relaxation: you need to achieve a state of relaxation, empty your brain of imagination and attention to the immediate world, and not strain towards the goal;
2. Expectancy: at the same time you need what might be called a state of "patient expectancy", where you are alert, attentive to the images about to arise from your unconscious without making a conscious effort;
3. Release: a sense that is like a charge of energy, a relief of tension;
4. Response: a sense of knowingness without engaging the conscious mind; at this point it is important to stay with the first impressions without attempting interpretation. They may be fragments of form or complete objects, and as you resist effort, with a true vision, you get a "hunch", the quality of which is described as a feeling of joy, a quality of brightness, vividness or compulsion (White, 1964).

Psychics tested and interviewed by Elizabeth Mayer (Mayer, 2008) used terms like "relaxed focus", "receptiveness", "no effort state of mind" "it's not me but it is" to describe the state they needed to achieve. Rosalind Heywood sees it as passive awareness, on the fringe of the mind, an inner prompting, an order that might appear absurd (Heywood, 1964); Polish psychic priest Father Klimuszko also talks of an internal command, some kind of "order" that he cannot resist (Klimuszko, 1989, p. 70).

Joe McMoneagle (McMoneagle, 2000, pp. 178-9) describes the experience in more scientific and philosophical terms, as achieving an altered state of consciousness, suspension of the intellect, focused awareness – a state similar to the mental and spiritual state of Zen, helped by use of meditation and hypnosis to increase openness to incoming information. But he also talks about "opening" to the target that produces the impression of a "quick taste" – a word, a picture, a thought, a sudden sensation that needs to be "re-tasted" a number of times, with other "tastes" appearing that in combination begin to produce an overall concept. The rest is "internalized processing", determining whether and how the taste is important (pp. 115-124).

Shielding of some kind from "noise" is something that successful clairvoyants have long done intuitively, using a variety of methods. Remote viewers talk about learning to dissociate from external input; Ossowiecki used to ask those present not to think about the task as this could give him a false lead (Barrington et al., 2005, p. 19) and "block" him, but instead to talk among themselves, helping him to calm his mind. Krzysztof Jackowski, the clairvoyant discussed in this volume, wants to know only the name of the person he is tracing (avoiding what is called "front-loading" in remote viewing), and seeks out noisy impersonal situations to distract himself while he waits for the flash of intuition. Psychics also have ways and rituals that help them to enter a special state. Alexis Didier had to be hypnotised to achieve clairvoyance, and many mediums need to enter some kind of trance to perform; for others a ritual or a device facilitates the process. Dowsing clearly works for some people, as demonstrated in Mayer's story of her daughter's precious stolen harp. In desperation, she took a friend's advice and contacted a dowser in a distant city who gave the harp's precise location by focusing on a map of the city where Mayer lived; not surprisingly, it changed her outlook on life (Mayer, 2008, pp.2-3). Crystal gazing may be somewhat unfashionable now but is another way of achieving a state of relaxed expectancy.

While the virtuosi's ability to focus on what is relevant to the task is remarkable and their hits are a long way beyond coincidence, the process itself is complex, fragmented and confusing. The conscious mind can become disoriented, mixing messages from the target with its own memories, associations, emotions, as well as picking up additional or unwanted information that might be associated with the target. In one of the experiments with Ossowiecki (Barrington et al., 2005, pp. 45-46, 50-51), he immediately picks up the target, correct personal information about the person who created the target, some embarrassment, and an aspect of the target that was not visible[30].

---

[30] The doctor who brought the target to the event in Paris had it created by a patient while he himself was absent. It was a piece of writing in a package sealed with two seals and the patient used a frank coin to seal it but the

The form in which the information arrives also varies both with the target and the clairvoyant (including mediums and their 'controls'); it involves different senses and may take the form of images, words, or sensations, be vague or specific, varying from person to person. Rosalind Heywood, talking about her spontaneous experiences, says, "A telepathic signal, for instance, can emerge to consciousness as a waking exterior hallucination, a sensation, an inner voice or image, a dream, a scent, or a simple urge to action ..." (Heywood, 1964 pp. 44-46, 60). We should also bear in mind that being in a special state may mean a loosening of sense of personal identity, of connection to reality, something reported both by Ossowiecki and Rosalind Heywood. And some clairvoyants describe what sounds like a personal visit to the intended location or object. Alexis Didier wrote, "I can transport from a pole to another with the speed of lightning; I can talk with the Cafres, walk in China, descend on the mines of Australia ..." (Alvarado, 2015), which seems to imply an out-of-body experience. Ossowiecki talks about trying to recreate the object or person in his imagination, and once that is achieved he moves "further and further into the cosmos of the universe" (...) it is enough to pick up an object, and instantaneously it transports me to those places on which I am concentrating" (Barrington et al., 2005, pp. 18-19). Remote viewers such as Pat Price and Joe McMoneagle, as well as Stefan Ossowiecki, describe looking down on locations and then descending into them, but perhaps that is more a question of language not being "designed" to report such experiences.

While true impressions come as a "hunch" or "inspiration", the interaction with the target can go way beyond what was intended. When he "visits" what turns out to be a submarine being built underground, Joe McMoneagle "knows" the function of the strange object he is "viewing" (which turns out to be a new and unusual type of submarine)[31]; in a number of investigations Ossowiecki refuses to name the culprit because he "knows" there would not be another offence; in the story of Elizabeth Mayer's stolen harp, found for her by a dowser located in

---

doctor, embarrassed at the common nature of the seal, superimposed on it a seal with images of Chaldean priests which completely covered the original imprint of the coin. Yet Ossowiecki "saw" the coin.

[31] The story of Joe McMoneagle's remote viewing of the Typhoon submarine is extremely well documented. "Copies of nearly all the original documents that still exist became available when the CIA publicly released the Star Gate project's archives in 2004" (Smith, 2016).

another city, the dowser claims to influence the thief not to cause damage to the instrument (Mayer, 2008, p. 263). Since some experiments with Ossowiecki involve influencing people to perform certain acts without their being aware of it (clairvoyant hypnosis?) we should perhaps look for further evidence rather than dismiss such claims.

However, detailed accounts of what seem simple experiments provide a more confusing picture of unexpected limitations. There is clearly a mixture of pathways through which information arrives, as in an experiment conducted by Richet with Ossowiecki (Barrington et al., 2005, pp. 40-41). The target is a few lines of text in a sealed envelope, but its meaning is complex. Having described the precautions against the possibility of leakage, and being unaware of the content himself, Richet spends an hour and a half with Ossowiecki, who, after setting the scene of the writing of the text in terms "not beyond the scope of ordinary good sense", has much difficulty with parts of the target:

"Life. Life. Life. (He repeats this word three times). There are four or five lines, and beneath that the signature Sarah Bernhardt, a signature that slopes upwards." ...

"Life seems humble ... life and humanity, but the word humanity is not written. There is an idea that is linked to the idea of life and humanity ... because there is a lot of hatred ... No, it is not hatred; there is only ... only ... it's a very difficult word, a very French word that I do not know: it's a word of eight letters. Exclamation."

The final version of Ossowiecki's reading was "Life seems humble because there is only hatred (not hatred, but a word that is not understood and which has eight letters; signature Sarah Bernhardt." The actual message was: *Life seems good to us, because we know it to be ephemeral!* [éphémère – eight letters – in French] – *Sarah Bernhardt.*

This is a puzzling and fascinating mixture of groping towards the meaning, and partly relying on the visual appearance of the text. Ossowiecki was fluent in French, so he gets the meaning of "life", but "ephemeral" might easily be unfamiliar to him, being somewhat literary. This seems to point to the conclusion reached by some writers on mediumship, that successful transfer of information depends on what is available in the medium's mind. The report also shares characteristics with the experience of Joe McMoneagle in an experiment where the remote viewers were aiming only to 'get' specific words: "What I noticed most about the experiment was the fact that the 'idea' conveyed by the word was transferred as information, not the individual letters. In other words, I wasn't seeing individual letters; I was seeing images in my mind" [the word 'flies' generates images of birds flying, planes taking off, insects hovering] (McMoneagle, 2006, pp.190-1).

In another experiment with Ossowiecki, this one with Geley, the psychic gives an exact description of the layers of packaging holding the target but never 'gets' the target, two fish scales. He does, however, describe something very small and thin that can be used like glass, which is close enough in appearance. Carp scales are an obscure target, but this experiment took place while Geley and Ossowiecki went fishing and spent some hours together (Barrington, 2005, pp. 58-9). Perhaps the process of interpreting the target falls in the domain of logical, so to speak left-hemisphere thinking, and Ossowiecki used a familiar concept closest to the image he perceived. But he could have "fished" for information in Geley's mind yet that never happened.

On the basis of remote viewing evidence, and many cases like the ones above, Joe McMoneagle is clearly right when he says that information need not be collected from inside the agent's head. Yet, since it is also the case that clairvoyance is goal-oriented and, again according to McMoneagle, "remote viewing uses whatever lines of communication or information resources are available" (McMoneagle, 2006, pp. 234-5, 154), in the case of fish scales the obvious available resource would seem to be telepathy with Geley's mind. Why does Ossowiecki describe the objects – small, flat and shiny – but cannot identify them? Geley is standing next to him and knows what they are. Maybe it is a question of too much focus on the wrong place in the truncated causal chain; maybe he is past the "roaming" stage and is now applying analytical faculties. This would imply lack of control over the levels of access. After all, alongside drawings, shapes, fragments in clairvoyance, we also have some spectacular examples of telepathy.

An illustration of the richness of the imagery linked to the target and its symbolic and associative nature is provided by the "receiver" in a ganzfeld telepathy experiment from 1980, who talks about "images of flames", "flames again", fire very menacing", "recently formed volcano", "molten lava inside the crater ... running down the side", "I think of water as a way of putting out flames ... biting my lip ... as though lips had something to do with the imagery". The "sender" was viewing a picture of two fire-eaters. (Williams, 2016, pp. 5-6)

Clairvoyance all around?

When you look at the different ways, different people, different descriptions and different routes by which information arrives through truncated causal chains, perhaps access is not as limited as it might appear. Perhaps most of us would not recognise clairvoyance because it is Carpenter's "first sight", quietly and unspectacularly operating all the time. We do not look for it unless experimenting or, as the US army did, hoping to apply it.

As has been said, most of us seem to have access to a rudimentary psi sense that may give rise to "hunches" or "gut feelings". It also seems to help if you have a creative personality; in telepathy experiments "in 128 Ganzfeld sessions with artistically gifted students at the University of Edingburgh, a 47 percent success rate was obtained, with odds of 140 million to one. Similarly, in a session with 20 undergraduates from New York's Juilliard School of performing arts, the students achieved a hit rate of 50 per cent" (Taylor, 2018, p. 154). We may also all be capable of performing better if we are shielded from environmental stimuli, as were the unselected participants placed in the ganzfeld condition, who performed significantly above chance (Roe et al, 2020).

There is a parallel here with physical, psychokinetic experiences. In studies of micro-PK, where the task was to affect random machine processes, what was important for success was "not the physical proximity of the machine but its proximity in terms of meaning. The successful subjects mentioned " ... a sense of 'resonance' or 'bond' with the machine; ... of 'falling in love' with it; of 'having fun' with it" (Roll, 2003, p. 84).

In his book *Selection effect* (Mertz, 2020) Herb Mertz[32] describes months of effort to achieve the skewing of the pattern of green or red dots on his REG to over a million to one odds – his own personal project. He analyses in detail the ebb and flow of success and failure and its relationship to his mental states, gaining personal confidence in creating a mental state conducive to success. What eventually happens is that he "gives up" trying, appeals to the universe and, as he puts it, creates a "connected self", not a brain self. He then achieves odds of 1.7 million to one. The way he explains it is that our brains set up expectations,

---

[32] Mertz has a background in engineering, and was involved in developing the famous PEAR project using Random Event Generators (REG) on an enormous scale.

boundaries of what is possible and normal. We have a "mental regulator" of expectations, "mental membranes", too deep for us to be conscious of them, that kick in when, for example, the run of hits is too successful. This is all to do with habituation, with the models of reality created on the basis of what usually happens. New goals (such as skewing REG patterns) are not the norm, they conflict with the usual subroutines that have a life of their own, and what you have to do is to shift the norm, affect your own state of mind to expect the abnormal.

Mertz is talking about PK in terms of breaking down boundaries, of intention; in clairvoyance we also talk of intention and becoming "one with the target". There is a continuity between psychokinesis, clairvoyance and roaming in the unconscious. And that leads to larger questions, those to do with mediumship, including physical mediumship.

Clairvoyants do not know where the information, the "taste" or the "order" comes from, and the same applies whether the targets are as yet non-existent, or photos, persons, or simple cards or numbers. Stimulus and response are interconnected by an unknown mechanism, the "truncated causal chains"; but in mediumship we have the added complication of the stimulus or response supposedly originating in a transcendent area, which may or may not be part of the unconscious. In other words, they may come from what appear to be conscious beings who no longer have a body – the discarnates.

5

CLAIRVOYANCE, MEDIUMSHIP
AND THE QUESTION OF SURVIVAL

~

Survival of death or living agent psi?

T he problem of the origin of the information applies to research into the possibility of survival of bodily death, where messages produced by mediums and interpreted as coming from the dead can also be seen as evidence of telepathy or clairvoyance, with the information coming from the minds of the sitters, or from outside sources accessed by the medium. This is known as super-psi or the living agent psi (LAP) hypothesis. Braude defines super-psi as "repeatedly accessing very specific often obscure information from multiple sources" (Braude, 2003, p. 86). According to that hypothesis, since we do not know how powerful psi can be in living persons, information might be obtained by searching through all possible sources in the world, from other minds to library archives. On the other hand, and on the view promoted by Braude and adopted here, possible messages from the discarnates would also require powerful psi (telepathy, clairvoyance or PK where the medium takes on the features/behavioural traits of the discarnate) for communication to be possible. So the assumption that clairvoyance is fundamental to all communication does not solve the question of where the information however obtained originates.

Since the beginning of psychical research, clairvoyance (including telepathy) and mediumship have converged and confused investigators. Volumes have been written on the subject of the possibility of survival of bodily death, but, however convincing the evidence, the Living Agent Psi hypothesis is a constant challenge since we do not know what psi is capable of. It may seem unlikely that a medium should be able for example, to search obscure archives, but, since distance and time are no obstacles to clairvoyance by the living, and the main factor is intent, no amount of detail provided in a sitting can be regarded as proof that the information is coming from the surviving psyche of a discarnate. Moreover, how else could the postulated discarnates communicate if not through clairvoyance? How else could they be aware of what is happening in the physical world now while not having a physical body (Braude, 2020, pp. 200-204)?

On the view that clairvoyance is fundamental the problem does not disappear, but perhaps a clearer picture might emerge if we do not attempt to establish dividing lines between clairvoyance and mediumship.

Historical background

Survival of bodily death was one of the topics of great interest to early investigators, partly because of the implications of scientific discoveries and theories (such as evolution) for religion, and partly because of the rise of Spiritualism and the mediumistic phenomena that it made popular. In the 1850s the craze for "table-tipping" arrived from the US, spread throughout Europe, and became a popular pastime regardless of social class. In mainstream view this phenomenon is easily explained by unconscious muscular movements of the sitters who have their hands on the table, but in order to take that view one needs to ignore the abundant evidence for tables (or other furniture) moving, responding to questions and almost acquiring personalities without anybody touching them. This phenomenon, of obtaining information through inanimate objects, is usually put down to the influence of sitters' unconscious telepathy/clairvoyance. However, that simply adds another level of inexplicability to the "truncated causal chains" of clairvoyance and, partly because it tends to take place in private circles, even psychical researchers have mostly ignored it[33].

From the start, mediumship was beset by unrealistic claims and by fraud. This particularly affected physical mediumship, with sittings in the dark, enthusiastic sitters keen to believe, and the difficulty of recording events. After unmasking many claimants, the SPR turned away from physical phenomena, but over the years found a number of mental mediums who produced relevant information under good controls. Concentrating on the question of survival, where people try to contact their deceased relatives and friends through mental mediums, was linked to the growth of Spiritualism, and this was particularly strong in English-speaking countries. French investigators took a more secular approach, while, in a deeply Catholic country like Poland, trying to contact the dead would have been regarded as a sin by the church and by devout Catholics, and dabbling in the occult would be frowned upon[34].

However, the dividing lines between psychometrists, clairvoyant mediums and trance mediums were (and still are) unclear. The séances held by early investigators were very personal, rich in detail, with the alleged discarnates sometimes reproducing the behaviour, language and mannerisms of the deceased personality through the medium. One of the most famous mental mediums who was investigated in depth and over a long time by the luminaries of the early period of psychical research was Leonora Piper. She was "discovered" by William James, the great American psychologist, via members of his household in 1885, and held sittings for investigators until 1910. Accounts of these sittings provide insights into a variety of aspects of clairvoyance, regardless of how one interprets the evidence.

Mrs Piper was a "trance medium," able to enter a state when she was insensitive to external stimuli. She provided information through speech, sometimes imitating the behaviour of the deceased communicator, sometimes employing psychometry, and in the later period mainly through automatic writing. Like many mediums, she had

---

[33] One example of such phenomena taking place today is to be found in Ann Treherne's *Arthur and me* (2020). Experiments were undertaken by Kenneth Batcheldor (Wehrstein, 2018).

[34] Teofil Modrzejewski, better known in psychical research as Franek Kluski the physical medium, initially welcomed scientific investigations but eventually ceased sittings as they veered towards trying to produce apparitions of the dead.

"controls", entities which acted as intermediaries between the sitters and communicators. Today, mediums claim to have "guides" rather than "controls" who seem to act as guardians or doorkeepers, allowing in some entities and not others. They are usually regarded as secondary personalities of the medium. Maria Przybylska, one of the clairvoyants mentioned earlier, also had a control who was called Vittorino, and who "told" her what she needed to know, often precognitively, but there were no known attempts at contact with the dead.

Mrs Piper's performance varied greatly in quality, often within the same trance. As in mediumship today, there was much emphasis on names, and there were clairvoyant statements about living relations and friends, as well as those who had died. Here also it is difficult to eliminate telepathy as the source of the medium's knowledge; however, sitters commented on her awareness of things that were far from their minds at the time of the sitting, as if accessing memories buried deep in the stream of consciousness.

There were some stunning "hits", reports of contemporary events, recognition of old friends, appropriate emotional responses, relating events not known to the sitter but to a friend or relative who confirmed the details on being contacted (such as the sitter's brother having been caught in a storm with the discarnate friend, staying in a strange, dirty hotel and making a joke of it) (Gauld, 2022, p. 106). Such trivia provide most convincing evidence of identity; but we also have examples where the medium provides much accurate detail about a person who later turns out to be living. Rosalind Heywood describes a case of accurate "fishing in consciousness" involving an anonymous sitting when she mentally asked about a friend whose fate was unknown to her. The discarnate friend made contact at the sitting, gave personal details, acted in character, and recounted many pleasant shared experiences. Since the friend was German and this was just after the end of the Second World War, Rosalind feared for his life and indeed the discarnate said that he had been killed in grim circumstances. Except that he hadn't – Rosalind traced him afterwards and found him living happily in a neutral country. Presumably both the friend's very convincing personality and his grim fate were constructed by the medium from Rosalind's memories and fears (Toynbee et al., 1968, p. 233). We also have cases of non-existent discarnates produced at the suggestion of the investigators, perhaps a mixture of clairvoyantly sourced information and confabulation, as if the medium's intention to find a target takes flight and meanders without clear direction.

So, while the main effort of mental mediumship is often aimed at establishing the identity of the communicator, verifiable information is always susceptible to being interpreted as telepathy and clairvoyance among the living, driven by the psychic's intention to obtain relevant information regardless of the source.

From highly personal to statistical

Research into the possibility of survival pretty much ground to a halt in the first half of the 20th century[35]. Original research involved person-to-person sittings, and the best sessions were arranged with proxy sittings (where a substitute takes the place of the person who wants to make contact with a discarnate), with notes being taken by another. The best mediums under the best controls provided data rich in personal detail that, however interpreted, forces one to consider a paranormal source of information.

However, such series of sittings could always attract charges of inadequate controls. Even after eliminating the obvious possibilities of fraud or cold reading (where the sitter unconsciously provides clues through appearance, responses and body language), leakage of information and bias in observation and reporting may play a role in interpreting what took place. Particularly, in series of sittings involving the same people over a period, their evidential value may diminish because of unconscious clues.

---

[35] The problem of identity and continued personality of discarnate communicators, capable of intelligent and intentional activity in afterlife, at times seemed to be solved through what is known as "the cross-correspondences". In 1903, after the death of Frederic Myers, different mediums, on different continents, began to receive partial messages, via automatic writing. These messages only made sense when put together by the intended recipients who, unlike the mediums, had the necessary knowledge to understand the sophisticated allusions to classical texts. When messages started coming from other deceased SPR founders as well, they gave the impression of a group working together and some researchers, especially those who had known the "authors" of the messages in life, came to regard them as authentic. However, most of these "cross-correspondences" were very complex, involved a number of communicators on both sides, and went on for a long time, so that the possibility of clairvoyance and other channels of information being involved could not be eliminated.

Today, some of the most technically sophisticated experimental research eliminates these drawbacks, and uses structured procedures susceptible to statistical analysis. Julie Beischel's experiments (Beischel, 2013, 2014, 2017) at the Windbridge Institute (founded in 2008) employed proxy sittings on a very complex and sophisticated level.

The mediums who took part in the Windbridge experiments were all practitioners who had been successfully tested for their psi ability. They were randomly matched with the sitters seeking contact with their departed. All contact between the sitter and the medium took place on the telephone via a proxy who only knew the name of the person that the sitter was trying to contact. The mediums were asked to describe their target's appearance, personality, interests, cause of death, or anything else that they picked up (often these would be emotional experiences of the person they were trying to contact). The conversations were recorded, transcribed and given to the sitters to judge how far the information corresponded to their knowledge of the person they were trying to contact. However, the sitters were given more than one transcript to rate (with some "decoy" ones) and had to identify the one that best applied to them. Most chose the one meant for them. Here, also, most mediums intuited correctly whether the target person was alive or dead.

This was a small study of 21 mediums, all American, mostly female, acting in a secular context. Many claimed that they could differentiate between survival psi and clairvoyance, and that it was the discarnates who "found" the right sitters once the medium "tuned in". (Beischel, 2017, p. 174). Some described the feeling as "merging", experiencing the discarnate person's emotions and personality, that could come through in a variety of ways: awareness of presence, a dreamlike state, or being "taken over" by the discarnate entity: there seems to be a continuum of experience.

However, if clairvoyance is the basic form of communication, obtaining information in inexplicable ways does not constitute evidence that it originated with discarnate entities, and Julie Beischel, the project director, does not make this claim. Also, the main purpose in mediumship seems to be to identify the communicator and establish continuity of their existence rather than to perform any specific task. You might say that the communicator is the target, with the intention of the living sitters and the medium entangled in the process alongside the content of their unconscious.

As has been said, gifted clairvoyants are rare, and intuitive awareness arrives through an "enormously complex web of interactions, psi and non-psi, overt and covert, local and global" – a "crossfire of underlying psychic activities" (Braude, 2003, p. 87, 92). In such circumstances, errors are easily made especially if, as many mediums claim, the departed can only make use of what is in the medium's mind. And it's not just the intuitive aspect of the process; in clairvoyance, whatever the source, interpretation is necessary so this is, at least, a two-stage process: acquiring information remotely, from another mind or a physical state, followed by responding to it, shaping it in a way that can be communicated in physical terms, through language, drawing, gesture and sound. It may involve misinterpreting, modifying, focusing on elements and introducing personal imagery or no imagery: in fact, a true "cognitive cocktail" (Braude, 2003 p. 253).

Motivated psi

Better kind of evidence for survival would be "motivated psi hypothesis" (Braude, 2020, p. 184), showing that the needs being satisfied are not those of the living but something still relevant to the discarnates; that the communicator has an agenda and initiates clairvoyant contact. It would also demonstrate *continuing awareness of, and interaction with, the physical world* (Braude, 2020, p. 203), by responding in appropriate manner to the appropriate living communicators and their situation. In other words, we need evidence of discarnate *intent*.

Unfortunately, in experiments the intent comes from the experimenters and participants, while the assumed discarnates are the target. But there are accounts where the intent seems to come from somewhere else: spontaneous cases and "drop-in communicators". The latter produce messages not aimed at making contact with anyone, but these messages turn out to be verifiable[36].

We also have accounts of spontaneous cases that are less spectacular but closer to the kind of inter-human encounters we are familiar with:

---

[36] In a private circle, messages from the ouija board turned out to be coherent, independently verifiable and very difficult to interpret in terms of random super-psi. They were not aimed at contact with anybody in particular but seemed intended to establish the communicators' identities, almost as if someone passing by saw an interesting party of strangers and was anxious to introduce himself. The most convincing aspects are where the communicator provided correct information while the published version was incorrect (37 drop-ins to a circle 1937-1964) (Gauld, 1971)

they have a clear purpose, and demonstrate the ability to remember, plan and perform (organise) things not possible in this life. Such an account comes from Russell Targ, physicist and one of the originators of remote viewing. It concerns his daughter Elisabeth, who was a mind/body researcher as well as a Russian translator. She died of a brain tumour at the young age of 40. A week after her death her husband was sent a letter by a nurse who had worked with Elisabeth. The nurse had a dream in which Elisabeth dictated to her a few words, one syllable at a time, for the nurse to copy and send on. Neither the nurse nor Elisabeth's husband knew what the groups of syllables meant, but Targ recognised it as two lines of Russian which, translated, simply said "I see you" and "I adore you". As Targ says, "If the nurse had simply spoken the English sentences to Mark on the phone, we would not be relating this story. It required the imagination of Elisabeth, who was a fluent Russian speaker, to find a unique way to communicate so as to send a message that would be understood as unambiguously from her." (Targ, 2012, 194-195; Katra, 2017). In its own way, this is a perfect case: a simple emotional message using a skill (knowledge of a specific foreign language) that identifies the departed intelligence, delivered by a third party. Such examples are few, but perhaps few are made public. We also have other well-documented reports of dreams in which the dreamer is urged to take action involving a third party. The famous medium Eileen Garrett who established the Parapsychology Foundation had a dream in which the deceased psychic investigator, Hereward Carrington, urged her to take care of his widow who needed help. As no action was taken, the following night she had the same visitor in a dream, this time very angry. The Foundation staff set out to track down Carrington's widow through psychical researchers in England, eventually found out her last known address, contacted the local police pretending to have heard something was wrong there, and saved the widow who had fallen and broken her hip three days earlier (LeShan, 2009, p.2). This is psychic detection where the detecting seems to be initiated by a discarnate: one who is aware of what is currently happening in the physical world. A number of other examples can be found in popular but reliable publications (such as Robertson, 2013), but there is one well documented case where a murder victim seems to take matters into her own hands. This account was published in the *Journal of the Society for Psychical Research* under the title "A possibly unique case of psychic detection" (Keen & Playfair, 2004)[37]. This was the case of a medium, Christine Holohan, who claimed that she was "made" to contact the police by a discarnate murder victim who appeared to her and demanded justice.

The murder took place in 1983. Christine was training to be a medium and had had psychic experiences for years. The murdered girl, Jacqui Poole, appeared (as a vision of "white energy of light", not an actual person) and provided sufficient details to enable Christine to go to the police. The policeman in charge was initially sceptical but as the interview went on he was shaken – Christine described Jacqui's friends and relations, the events of that evening, Jacqui's flat, the murderer, the murder, the murderer's nickname, but there was nothing that could not have been obtained naturally. What shook them was when Christine took one of the detective's keys and told him personal details (such as a letter about essential electrical work), one of which was too personal and accurate to give to the researchers.

The suspect was released for lack of evidence, but in 2000 the case was reopened when DNA evidence became available through the use of new technology, and the murderer identified by Christine was convicted.

Apart from the story itself, what made this case "possibly unique", was the extent to which the two psychic investigators provided its corroboration and context, with the collaboration of the two detectives who had been involved and who made available their original notes and comments. This is a rare occurrence in the area of collaboration between the police and psychics, to which we turn now.

---

[37] The case was reported in *Psychic News* under the headline "Medium catches killer and proves life after death", demonstrating the difference in scholarly vs popular approaches.

6

PSYCHICS, DETECTIVES AND PSYCHIC DETECTIVES

~

Inflated expectations

There are numerous challenges to claims of psychic detection, the primary one being the assumption that it cannot and, therefore, does not exist. Since most of this book so far has been devoted to demonstrating the presence of extrasensory perception, or some degree of psychic detection (clairvoyance) in the wider sense at the most fundamental level of existence, it would not serve any purpose to recapitulate the arguments at this stage. The only difference between the evidence presented earlier and the specific case studies which follow this introduction is that they take place in real life, are aimed at solving real life problems, often involve criminal activities, and above all are exceptionally well documented.

Cases where police forces turn to "psychic detectives", i.e. clairvoyants, are often surrounded by a febrile atmosphere of claims and counter-claims. Here we have extravagant claims of psychics "solving" crimes (with titles in the media such as "psychic solves murder case that had the police baffled"), official denials, as well as cases (usually quite horrific) that attract much media attention and a great number of calls to the police by psychic claimants – people who, usually wrongly, believe they have clairvoyantly received relevant information. And, of course, there are many frauds and charlatans.

Popular collections of cases, or (auto)biographies of psychics, some of them spiritualist mediums, often also claim to contribute to solving crimes, with the names and sometimes photographs of the police officers involved (Roberts, 1969; Jones, 1982; Boot, 1994; Robinson, 1997; Randles & Hough, 2001; Renier, 2008). They tend to tell the psychic's life story that includes accounts of helping the police. The significant details about the cases and the psychic's modus operandi usually convincingly fit in with what we know about how clairvoyance works. They tend to report involvement in highly sensational cases with their own spectacular success, but the cases often rely on impressions and memories of events that took place many years earlier. Unfortunately, even when they quote police confirmation, these are often unverified narratives by individuals, produced at unspecified times, without validation by official institutions. Perhaps the Skeptiko interview with Nancy Weber (Weber, 2008) represents a classic case of a story with no satisfactory ending: Nancy, a psychic and spiritualist medium, tells a dramatic story of how she identified a murderer and brought him to justice, guided by spirits who seem to have helped in the capture. Nancy drives the narrative and the police officers involved generally confirm her story, but by then are vague about the details and have thrown away their notes, while the case is some decades old. In the discussion, which ensues, there is thus no way of effectively countering the (sometimes quite reasonable) arguments of the representative of the sceptical point of view.

Dramatic stories of this kind told with conviction may also give rise to the unrealistic expectation that a psychic impression must be right; some psychics reinforce this expectation by having a strong belief in their own powers, or in their supernatural source, and the subject tends to drift towards what is vaguely referred to as the "occult", from palm readings at fairs to general prophecies (preferably of doom) beloved by the media. Yet, as has been said earlier, those with genuine experience of extrasensory access to information would never claim to be successful all the time, while their experiences tend to be impressions, flashes of intuition, multisensory images, and usually not spectacular visions. The famous psychic Ingo Swann made the important point that "There is a great misconception about how ESP *should* work. The expectation is that it should be present along some kind of reproducible, mechanistic lines – when in fact it is a human ability present at its ultimate only if a lot of other things are present … I know of no human ability that is ideally present all the time; yet the attitude is prevalent that if a psychic is successful one time, he or she ought to be equally successful on demand" (Lyons & Truzzi, p. 188). This message clearly does not resonate with the media or the public who are eager for sensational feats or failures.

Another challenge to psychic detection is the "standard" accusation against psychic statements, of being so vague and general as to be useless; such as claiming that the body is near water, or road, or trees. It is a fact that people generally tend to underestimate the probability that some "clues" apply to many situations and large segments of the population (one of the best-known examples is that more than a third of us have a scar on one knee, which makes a psychic's claim to that effect somewhat less impressive). On the other hand, it is also a fact that the world is full of landscapes with water, roads and trees and that means that a missing person who has not come back from a walk, will likely have gone missing against such a background. The extrasensory element will usually involve identifying a concatenation of individual characteristics of the relevant landscape, not just one item.

It is also important to bear in mind that in spite of the popular image, "psychic detectives" do not solve crimes. They only provide clues, which can sometimes be vital and can be used by the police or other bodies to do the actual detecting. Such clues may be the only ones available in cases where the police turn to psychics after all the possible normal clues have been explored and led nowhere.

Experimental evidence

It is generally acknowledged that psychic detection has fared poorly in controlled experiments (Wehrstein, 2019). This is what one would expect in a situation where the information comes spontaneously, fragmentarily and fuzzily and success depends on conducive conditions and perceptive interpretation suited to the individual. It is also a fact that in the few reported (and not recent) experiments, the methodology employed paid no attention to the main characteristics of the phenomenon. Some of the studies were not actually aimed at the issue of accuracy of psychic detection, but at such questions as the use of rhetoric by psychic claimants (O'Keeffe & Alison, 2000) or expertise in psychological profiling (Kocsis et al., 2000). One study used two self-declared psychics without validating their claims and a methodology that would have been quite alien to most practitioners (Baker et al., 2017), and the results were predictably negative. The obvious flaw of recruiting self-proclaimed psychic claimants rather than practitioners with a proven track record was avoided in an experiment by Wiseman et al. (1996). However, on this occasion, no account was taken of the psychics' usual methods of operating, such as getting psychic impressions in dreams and not through psychometry, as happened with one of the participants, Chris Robinson (Robinson, 2006). Also, perhaps inevitably, the experiments to date bear little relation to the pragmatic approach taken by police officers when they are trying to solve real-life crimes and problems.

The most recent review of research into psychic detection is that by Sybo Schouten (Schouten, 2021). He discusses a number of important cases and investigations, including the experimental and anecdotal ones, also with reference to Lyons & Truzzi (1991) and various small-scale studies and questionnaires carried out between the 1960s and 1990s. According to this review, most of the calls from members of the public turn out to be irrelevant, and the input from experienced psychics – predictably in the context of what we know about clairvoyance – tends to be variable. A four-year study of psychics' contributions to searches for missing persons suggested that "about 10% of the psychics will contribute something useful to the investigation and that about 3% will provide the correct solution" (Schouten, 2021, p. 211). However, how usefulness is assessed will vary depending on the individual police force's experience, so the data is not necessarily reliable. Schouten also makes the point that "failures tend to remain unpublished", so the ratio of successful contributions cannot be established (p. 212).

Inevitably, research into the use of extrasensory perception as an investigative method is also miniscule in Poland, and hardly reliable. Small-scale studies, such as by Gruza et al. (2008) make the familiar claim that the information provided by psychics is so general as to be useless, with nearly always the same elements of water, road and trees. There is also the suspicion that objects belonging to the person being sought that are given to the psychometrist also provide clues. The limited experiments carried out with psychics by these researchers also gave predictably unsuccessful results. In another study, a post-doctoral comparison of 12 clairvoyants' contributions, Krzysztof Jackowski came first, but the same problems crop up here as in the research into detection and ESP worldwide: lack of appropriate methodology and a shortage of comparative material, which makes assessment difficult (Janoszka, 2014, pp. 134-5). Successful psychics (and since they are so few you might call them statistical outliers in themselves), even if they keep records, concentrate on documenting their successes, and, in this respect, it is only the remote viewing procedures that provide a kind of standard. There, as has been said, a success rate of 50% would be regarded as high. On the other hand, Noreen Renier (Renier, 2008), a well-known American psychic, claims a success rate of 70-80% but no analysis of how that figure is achieved. Interestingly, though, her description of how she works is strikingly similar to that of Jackowski: she is a psychometrist who uses personal belongings to tap into the other person's thoughts or the energy left behind; she puts these belongings against her forehead to create the link, and talks of tuning in, merging the energies. Even though her accounts are first-person and somewhat sensationalised, they sound verifiable and deserving of further enquiry.

Anecdotal and other evidence

A comprehensive, objective and still relevant overview of real-life situations where psychics and police detection come together is to be found in *The Blue Sense: Psychic Detectives and Crime* (Lyons & Truzzi, 1991). The authors are aware of the varying degrees of credibility that should be attached to accounts, from varying sources, of the scarcity of proper documentation and the damage done to the subject by false accounts (they are particularly scathing about Peter Hurkos, a controversial psychic who was famous at one time as a stage and TV personality as well as a psychic detective) and self-promoting psychic claimants, but they also identify flaws in the studies available at that time (such as, for example, categorising unverifiable statements as incorrect) and do not dismiss less well documented cases out of hand. They are also aware of the individualistic methods – or perhaps rituals – adopted by different psychics, and of psychics "specialising" in aspects of clairvoyance, such as finding missing persons (or bodies), missing objects, archaeological sites, natural deposits etc. (Lyons & Truzzi, pp. 70-92). This sounds very much like the preferences established in studies of remote viewers discussed earlier.

The Blue Sense also provides accounts of a number of clairvoyants whose successes are confirmed by the police officers with whom they worked, such as Greta Alexander, Dixie Yeterian (p.2) or Florence Sternfelds, "a plump and warmhearted grandmother who worked with police without pay for over forty years" without seeking recognition

(p. 31). However, in a field where fraud, wishful thinking and distorted memory are a constant hazard, most such stories merge into a mass of "anecdotal reports" because of a lack of objective documentation, since police officers "rarely keep their notes of psychic tips" and this may result in the stories growing in the telling. The authors also point out that the police naturally tend to assess psychics in terms of how helpful their information was in solving the case, not how accurate their statements were (p. 140). Sometimes there are also problems when what seems like scholarly documentation turns out to be less than reliable, as happened with Dr Wilhelm H.C. Tenhaeff's books and articles on Gerard Croiset. Croiset achieved international fame and reputation as a wizard of clairvoyance, the best-authenticated psychic detective who "solved many of the century's most puzzling crimes, found scores of lost objects and hundreds of missing persons" and was an outstanding healer in the 1950s (Lyons and Truzzi, 1991, p. 93). There is plenty of evidence for Croiset's outstanding psi ability[38], but there is also evidence that "Dr Tenhaeff's recording is sometimes defective" (Zorab, 1965), while a number of Tenhaeff's tests were judged to be deeply flawed (Eisenbud, 1986; Hoebens, 1986). What made the evidence problematic was the fact that "...Tenhaeff generally acted as Croiset's publicist as well as scientific sponsor" (Lyons & Truzzi, 1991, p. 95), and his academic career seemed to be closely linked to his investigations of the clairvoyant's psychic abilities.

This is a cautionary tale of a conflict of interest; another tale relates to the problem of having access to reliable sources that affected even the authors of *The Blue Sense*. According to them, "Another Jew who was sought and eventually executed by the Nazis was Stefan Ossowiecki, who, it is claimed, used his paranormal powers to aid the Polish underground. Among his alleged psychic feats of wartime detection was the locating of specific bodies in mass graves." (Lyons & Truzzi, 1991, p. 197). Not one of these statements is accurate: Ossowiecki was not Jewish; he most probably died in a mass massacre of civilian population carried out by the Nazis after the Warsaw uprising in 1944; he did not work with the Polish underground, and there is just one documented case where he located a specific body in a mass grave. This is not to denigrate the research carried out by Lyons and Truzzi, but it does demonstrate the problems when access

---

[38] There is an exhaustive article on Croiset in *Psi Encyclopedia* by van Luijtelaar & Kramer, 2020; for a small but very detailed case see Zorab, 1965.

to primary sources is difficult, and underlines the importance of validating second-hand information.

Clairvoyants and the law

As has been said already, parapsychology has a problem with mainstream academia, even though it has become an academic subject itself. However, in real life, people tend to go with what works for them, especially when their options are limited, and this applies to police work as well. A rational discussion of the use of extrasensory perception in law enforcement and police investigation is thus especially relevant, because of the ethical and legal implications of using unorthodox methodologies. There are some publications in English, which discuss this question (Lyons & Truzzi, 1991), but, to date, such research has been scant. Accounts of the feats of psychic detection (often by the psychics themselves) tend to contrast with accounts of unsuccessful experiments (often by hostile academics), so it is rare to hear the views of "expert users" – people for whom clairvoyance is a methodology that has specific practical and legal implications.

One important aspect of Janoszka's research was an analysis of those criminal cases where the investigation was a success because of the information provided by Jackowski. The main aim was to establish the value of that data and the way in which it contributed to solving the case. At this stage of research Janoszka conducted interviews with the police officers who were directly involved in the investigations. He followed this by obtaining expert opinion on police procedures and the legal aspects of such collaboration.

The clairvoyant, Jackowski, made his wide-ranging documentation available for analysis. Interestingly, these documents talk about providing information, offering a version of events that correspond to the facts, or about providing clues as to how the crime took place, or to the location of the bodies, but in no case was the word "clairvoyance" used. This reflects the lack of clarity in the official and legal status of such information, very much as is the case in the West.

Some of Janoszka's interviewees, particularly those with practical experience of working with clairvoyants, made the point that collaboration by law enforcers with clairvoyants should be discussed and officially recognised instead of being kept secret from the superiors, thus avoiding unnecessary controversy such as Janoszka's battle for recognition of Jackowski's contributions. Another important point was that in some cases unconventional methods are essential, otherwise no progress can be made. Generally, the advice of officers who had worked with Jackowski and some other clairvoyants with a verified track record was to use common sense, to guard against suggestion, to bear in mind that a psychic's statement is not evidence, and not to initiate action, particularly where cost is involved, just on the basis of a psychic's claim. On the other hand, if you are searching a large area it can be cost-effective to employ a reliable psychic to narrow the search. However, it is vital to bear in mind that the information provided by a clairvoyant cannot be used as evidence. It may help in the investigation, but it is necessary to have the conventional evidence material.

This means that there can be a problem with establishing the legal status of evidence obtained through the use of clairvoyance. Alongside letters of confirmation and acknowledgment, there are documents calling Jackowski in for questioning as a witness (Janoszka, 2014, pp. 268, 273, 279, 289, 293), appointing him as an expert witness (pp. 264-5), and one warrant for his detention (p. 284) – fortunately revoked after Jackowski presented himself as a witness and explained how he knew where to find the body (Janoszka, 2014, p. 284). Such documentation reflects muddled legal thinking: an expert witness has special knowledge in a specific area; a psychic also has special knowledge but its source is not verifiable by current scientific methods; a psychic also cannot be a witness, not having physically witnessed the events, and providing information that leads to obtaining evidence without a rational account of the source of that information. The most satisfactory solution seems to be to grant the psychic the status of consultant, an advisory role relating to specific problems, on a confidential basis, at various stages of the process of investigation or prosecution. For the police, the important aspect of such advice or information is its effectiveness; its origin is not relevant. Collaborating with psychics on that basis should not be a problem for the police at any stage of their work, and should make it possible to ensure security and anonymity for the psychic. This is important as, being famous, Jackowski has been approached by criminals trying to learn whether they were being targeted by the police.

As has already been said, many published anecdotal accounts sound very similar to the cases where Jackowski made a contribution; psychics tend to become involved in searching for missing persons because this is something that happens quite frequently; like remote viewers, some psychics are better than others at specific tasks and tend to specialise;

they also tend to have their own ways, or rituals, of engaging with their ability that works for them. The main difference is that there are few who can provide objective documentation of their accounts.

A less obvious but quite important difference between many published accounts and Jackowski's cases is the minimal involvement of police resources and interaction. Generally speaking, all that happens is that the police or private individuals supply a relevant personal item relating to the person of interest; there is very little travelling together, or following the trail or personally directing the search, which tend to feature largely in stories of this kind. Thus, there are usually no conversations, and no opportunities to learn from hints or visual and other clues. What is important is to have the clairvoyant contribution documented as early as possible, to avoid misremembering.

Another feature of many cases involving Jackowski is that, while they may be sordid and brutal, they tend to lack spectacular features of interest to the public and the media, such as serial killers, celebrities, assassinations or terrorist plots. One Texan police officer comments about psychics: "They call you on sensational cases, not on cases where some wino is stomped to death in some back alley" (Lyons & Truzzi, 1991, p. 92). With Jackowski, the police often do consult him on the Polish equivalents of such unspectacular events.

Bearing in mind Jackowski's experience of how public bodies avoid references to clairvoyance while acknowledging his contribution, it is perhaps not surprising that successful involvement of psychics in general is unlikely to be made public, whether in Poland or elsewhere. However, there are a number of people in positions of authority, particularly those who have experienced working with him and with other psychics, who are prepared to testify to the existence of the phenomenon of clairvoyance and to Jackowski's abilities, and think that the subject deserves serious scientific discussion. Such is one of Janoszka's interviewees, Professor Ryszard Jaworski, Chair of Forensic Science Department at the University of Wrocław, who also makes the point that not all information about confirmed cases reaches the Police Headquarters and official statistics. Some contacts remain secret as part of the operational records. Another interviewee, a forensic expert and anthropologist with more than forty years' experience, confirms that he has worked with psychics (not on his initiative and only in relation to particular investigations) and knows of cases where detailed information from them made it possible to locate people or bodies.

Dr Mirosław Lisiecki, previously a police officer and now a university professor, who has researched the use of ESP in police work, is positive about using psychics and having an open mind about things we do not understand, but also stresses the need to verify psychics' claimed achievements, to be aware of the limits of their usefulness, and to be careful not to become part of a psychic's advertising. Having successfully worked with Jackowski as a police officer himself, Lisiecki confirms that he had never given the clairvoyant any "courtesy" testimonials. He deplores the fact that most psychics do not document their activities so that they cannot be verified, and praises Jackowski's record keeping, which he finds totally credible (Janoszka, 2014).

So it is likely that many cases simply disappear under the radar. Sybo Schouten describes one exceptional case of a "psychic policeman" who takes part in a search for a missing teenager and whose strikingly accurate statements regarding the girl's locations are documented by the other police officers involved in the search, but his general conclusion is: "I do not know of any anecdotal case in which a psychic, only by handling an object related to a crime about which he or she had no further information, was able to correctly identify the perpetrator" (Schouten, 2021, p. 230). But in some of the cases to be recounted now, Jackowski does exactly that: he correctly identifies the perpetrator by handling an object related to a crime without any further information.

7

KRZYSZTOF JACKOWSKI, JOE MCMONEAGLE AND STEFAN OSSOWIECKI: KINDS OF CLAIRVOYANCE – KINDS OF CLAIRVOYANTS

~

The value of case studies

A case study "often involves an intensive examination of a specific issue and/or individual or event ... it has been suggested that more discoveries have emerged from using case studies than from relying on statistical analysis of large samples" (Vernon, 2021, pp. 12-13). The selection of studies presented in this chapter include a number of cases from Jackowski's dossier, chosen as representative of his kind of clairvoyance, and a number of impeccably documented cases from two other clairvoyant "virtuosi" as comparative material. Jackowski's cases are a small fraction of his dossier, and they are not presented in chronological order. Instead, we start with a case that may be the most remarkable in the range of aspects of clairvoyance it demonstrates, followed by an interview with the police officer involved, quoted in full.

Krzysztof Jackowski

Case 1: *Murder with roots in the past, 2006*
Location: Będzin (Silesian Highlands, southern Poland)
Case summary:

In the winter of 2006 the fire brigade was called out to a fire in a block of flats at a street in the town of Będzin, in southern Poland. The firemen succeeded in putting out the fire and preventing the whole building from being destroyed. One flat was badly damaged by the fire, the one inhabited by the owner of the block.

When the firemen and the police examined the damaged flat they made a macabre discovery: in the kitchen there were two charred bodies. The post-mortems showed that in both cases death was caused not by fire but by knife wounds. There was no doubt that the two people were murdered before their bodies were set on fire.

Investigation of the circumstances of this crime was not getting anywhere. Various hypotheses were explored but all came to a dead end. Finally, three investigating officers from Będzin undertook the long journey from Silesia to Człuchów (Jackowski's home town in Pomerania, in north-western Poland). On arrival they presented the clairvoyant with bags of scorched rags, tied and secured but still with the smell of burning emanating from them. After an initial blankness, with the bags in the room, Jackowski got what he calls a "vision":

He has an impression of a shop, a tiny shop with paints, owned by a young married couple. There is also a young girl there, employed as a trainee. The shop appears to be in the same block where the killing took place. Jackowski senses that the murderer is the man who manages the shop. He also becomes aware that the man has left his wife and is living with the trainee who worked in the shop. They were having an affair; the wife found out about it and that was the main reason for their splitting up. Another impression he has is that it all happened much earlier than the murder – something like two or three years.

Jackowski then makes a note: the trainee knows that the shop manager killed the owner of the block and the other victim, a tenant. The clairvoyant suggests that the trainee should be the first to be interrogated.

When he reads out his notes to the policemen they do not believe him. None of it makes sense; his stories have nothing to do with the investigation. There is no shop in that block; it's an old, dilapidated building. After the session, the police officers told Jackowski that there were quite a few homeless people always trying to spend the night in the cellar, and the owner kept calling the police to get rid of them. The police knew quite a lot about the homeless and were pretty certain it was one of them but they were a very closely-knit group so there were no clues (Świątkowska & Jackowski, 2012, vol 1 p. 136).

Disappointed, the policemen depart leaving the clairvoyant feeling guilty about his failure.

A few days later, when he was beginning to get over that unfortunate episode, one of the policemen from Będzin telephoned him and told him that he was right. The police checked out his story and it turned out that three years earlier there had been a little shop with paint in that block, run by a married couple, and they had a girl trainee. The police located the wife of the ex-shop manager, who told them that her husband turned out to be a scoundrel, they were divorced, and her former husband was living in a village with their ex-trainee, who had a child by him. When the police went to that village and started interrogating the girl she admitted almost at once that her partner told her what happened, that he did not intend to kill the old woman. He owed her money and she threatened to take him to court, so he went to her to try to come to some agreement. Instead, they had an argument, he got upset, hit the old woman on the head with something and she fell down. At that moment a tenant from a neighbouring flat came in to find out what all the screaming was about and was also dispatched.

The decision to ask Jackowski for help was taken by the then district chief of police in Będzin, Insp. Dariusz Brandys and his second-in-command, Insp. Zbigniew Klimus, who later became first deputy chief of police in the voivodship of Katowice, and recounted the case as follows:

In January 2006 a block of flats in Będzin was set on fire; after the fire was extinguished two bodies were found, and the post-mortem established that these were the owner of the block and her tenant," explained Klimus in the monthly "Policja 997" (June 2013). "Their injuries pointed to homicide, but there was no motive. The investigation dragged on and we had done everything we could, so I decided to use a clairvoyant. My superiors were not too happy about it, but I was confident in my decision." The police went to Człuchów with objects that had belonged to the victims. Within a few hours the clairvoyant provided information about a witness, he told us to talk to the person whose location he gave us. The officers involved add: "We went there: the witness [i.e. Jackowski] said the girl was troubled by the knowledge she had. Thanks to the information from Krzysztof Jackowski the criminals were caught." According to Inspector Klimus, "Jackowski surprised the police officers who came to see him. He did not know whom to expect but he knew the policemen's names and told them precisely what their role was in the investigation. It is the job of the police to find the criminals, and how they do it is their business. (...) I was never ashamed of this collaboration and later on I also had help from the clairvoyant on a number of occasions.

WE WOULD NOT HAVE SOLVED THIS CASE WITHOUT JACKOWSKI

Based on Krzysztof Janoszka's interview with one of the police officers who visited Jackowski, Commissioner Edward Adamek, Superintendent of the District Criminal Investigations Department, Police Headquarters in Będzin, in 2017 (now retired).

In January 2006 there was a fire in Będzin, in a flat in an old apartment block, resulting (as initially thought) in the death of two people. However, it turned out that this was a case of arson, and the post-mortems showed that the bodies had incision wounds and craniofacial injuries, which meant that we were dealing with a double homicide.

The decision to seek help from Krzysztof Jackowski was taken by my then superior, Insp. Dariusz Brandys and his deputy Insp. Zbigniew Klimus. My attitude was very sceptical, all the more so since it was one of my last cases before retiring. Moreover, I am a non-believer, and that includes life after death. But on the other hand I thought, "What's the harm in trying?" I found out from the police station in Człuchów how to contact Jackowski and then I set out on the night journey to Pomerania (north-western Poland) with two other policemen. We got there early in the morning. And when I saw that clairvoyant, lighting one cigarette after another, I felt even more distanced from the whole enterprise, because I did not really believe in those abilities he was supposed to have.

When we started talking he drew a few lines and said, "I will throw a bit in here, and in here, and in here, but you with the knowledge you have will need to put it all together." He would give us the pieces of the puzzle and we were to put them together.

Jackowski did not even know where we were from. We only told him that we were from Silesia and it was the question of a killing. So, we gave him the clothes and photos of the victims. He smelled them and put them to his forehead. Every few moments he would get excited, get up, smoke and walk around the flat. It was all spontaneous. Suddenly he started explaining to us: "This killing has two aspects. At the beginning the perpetrators killed their victims, and then returned to remove the traces". And then he started saying something we did not understand. "I have this impression of some little shop, where the owners are a married couple. There is also a young woman there, a trainee. The husband was cheating on his wife with her. When she [the wife] found out she left him and he started living with that trainee in some village. He is the murderer. He owed some money to the owner of the block. His girlfriend knows all about it. I see a village and a white church eight kilometres from the place where the killing took place."

After I heard that I was totally mistrustful of his credibility and the point of our visit. What church, what eight kilometres from the murder scene? Some sort of windup! So I say: "mate, what the f... are you talking about?" And suddenly he says: "There, where there is this church, that woman lives there who will tell you all about it. She worked in that shop. Her lover is the one who did it."

Suddenly he says he is getting confused, takes a piece of paper and writes "Jaskół" on it. He then says: "That's the word that comes into my mind – Jaskóła, Jaskół. I don't know what this might be"? So I then say, "Krzysztof, next to me is sitting Jacek Jaskólski, the policeman who was the first at the crime scene". And then he said: "It's you, I am getting mixed up because of you!" I was surprised then, and we kept the piece of paper as a souvenir.

On our way back from Jackowski we were confused, but later on we saw a way forward because we established that there really had been a shop in that block, run by a married couple, and a young girl did work there. Where was she from? From Wojkowice Kościelne, some eight kilometres from Będzin. And there really is a characteristic white church there. We also established that the victim – the owner of the block – lived alone; her whole family lived in Canada. She also had an apartment in the Old Town district in Warsaw, so she was quite well off. The perpetrator rented the premises from her and was behind with the rent. He was supposed to vacate them by 1st January [2006].

We needed a plan of action. Back in Będzin we had a meeting in chief Brandys's office, with the chief and his deputy Insp. Zbigniew Klimus, later deputy police chief of the Katowice voivodship. We decided to put a plan into action in a few days' time. Three days later the police brought that girl from Wojkowice Kościelne and she told the full story. There was building work being carried out, and when she was in the toilet she heard through a plaster wall her partner and his friend arranging the murder[39]. They were discussing how to solve the problem. The man was keen to continue his business (by that time he was running a small bar there), but the owner of the block not only demanded the outstanding rent, but also wanted to terminate his lease. So he decided that the simplest solution would be to get rid of the woman. We then got into his computer and found he had recently been looking at "fires", "explosions" and such like.

His arrest was quite spectacular. We went with an antiterrorist unit to Iwonicz Zdrój, where he was having spa treatment. That's where we arrested him, and he confessed to everything. He then tried to pretend he was ill, but the medics would not confirm it and he was judged to be fit.

We made an operational note of our meeting with Jackowski but we said nothing about it in court because we would have been laughed out of that court. I don't even know whether the perpetrators know that it was because of him – or thanks to him – that they ended up in prison. It was Jackowski who made it possible for us to gather very strong evidence against them.

I used to be fairly sceptical about things like that, but after meeting Jackowski I came to believe that there must be something to it. There is no other option. Because – how could he have known about it? It could not have been coincidence or luck. How could he have known that the killing did not take place somewhere in a forest, only in a building where there was a shop on the ground floor? That the name of one of the policemen is Jaskólski? That eight kilometres from Będzin there would be a village, with a church, and the witness would be living there?

I live close to a church but I am not a believer. If I had not visited Jackowski personally I would never have believed it, even from the

---

[39] This account differs slightly from the summary of Jackowski's impression but, on checking, both versions are true; the perpetrator would present his role in the murder in the best possible light when explaining it to his girlfriend, the policeman concentrates on the main facts.

most trusted policemen. I would think they perhaps embroidered a little, perhaps some coincidence ... But I'd been there! F ... I see a bloke who says "Jaskół" and that if we go to see a woman who lives eight kilometres from the place where the killing took place she will tell us all about it and then we go to her, bring her to the station and she tells us everything, just as Jackowski said!

We never directed Jackowski in any way while we were there. He had no access to the case records, and got no clues from us. We only gave him the clothing and photographs of the victims. What's more, when he was looking at the photograph of the man he said that he was not the killers' target and that his death was accidental. Later it turned out that this was true. The man heard shouting and went to see what was happening. He was simply in the wrong place at the wrong time.

There is no possibility that Jackowski could have staged this whole story. If it had been a case that had been in the media then perhaps you might try to think up some scenario, but nobody knew about that killing then, not even in Będzin. To start with there was only news of a fire. But he gave us a witness – who it was and where to find her!

The police never admit officially to working with Jackowski. When I hear the spokesman from the police headquarters say that he does not believe that a clairvoyant helped and that the police do not work with people like that, I say, "Mate! What are you talking about, when you've only ever seen a corpse perhaps in formalin sometime in training! You were never at a crime scene! You have no idea what operational work is like and you talk that sort of crap? Or is that what you have been told to say?" I've come all the way from constable to chief inspector, so I do know a thing or two about it. Obviously, it sounds better when a case is solved by superb police investigation methods and not by using a clairvoyant. But sometimes you need to tell people the truth. Undoubtedly in my case Jackowski helped and I am convinced that he is capable of helping other policemen. He has many statements from the police confirming his help in solving cases from all over the country. They are real, not forced or conventional courtesies, in spite of what some try to claim.

Nobody blamed us for deciding to use Jackowski's help. Of course it was quite risky. I myself did not believe on the way there, but on the way back – I did. For solving this case Jackowski received from us thanks written by Chief Dariusz Brandys. I assure you he is not the kind of man who would have put his name to something that was not true, or some meaningless bit of paper. Although I admit that the acknowledgment was expressed somewhat diplomatically. It said that Jackowski helped us but in truth he solved the case for us.

The police have nothing to lose by collaborating with a clairvoyant. You become a policeman; you take on this job to solve cases; by what method? It doesn't matter. What is important is that it should be legal. If standard methods fail, why not use unconventional ones? It's no shame and no loss. Obviously, a clairvoyant will not serve the solution on a plate, telling you everything in detail and identifying the criminal by name. He will tell you something but the policeman investigating the case has to draw conclusions using that information himself.

Should I be ashamed that I worked with Jackowski? I'll be honest, I felt greatly honoured. We managed to put away two bastards who killed two people for the sake of two thousand zlotys [ca £500]. And that is not the only case where Jackowski helped! There are many of them! Even finding many missing persons – fathers, mothers, sons. Is it not a relief for the families to be able to bury their loved ones and get closure?

"Police press release about two killers being given a sentence of life imprisonment:
District Police Headquarters in Będzin."

LIFE SENTENCE FOR A KILLING FROM THREE YEARS AGO

The Regional Court in Katowice sentenced two residents of Będzin to life imprisonment, the highest sentence possible in Poland. In a circumstantial prosecution two men aged 28 and 29 were sentenced for a killing, which they carried out nearly three years ago on the night of New Year's Eve in 2005.

To recap: in the early hours of 2 January 2006 a fire started in one of the apartment blocks at Modrzejowska Street in Będzin. During the firefighting action the bodies of a woman and a man were found in two flats. It was established that the fire was started deliberately, and that the people had died earlier. Thanks to the efforts of the police in Będzin the probable course of events was established, and the perpetrators were identified and detained. The evidence gathered made it possible to take proceedings against them. They were also prosecuted for other crimes, i.e., bodily harm and threats.

The document reproduced below is the official statement thanking Jackowski and confirming his contribution in the case of the killing of Jadwiga S. and Tadeusz B. and arson at the apartment block, issued by the District Police Headquarters in Będzin, signed by the District Chief of Police in Będzin Insp. Dariusz Brandys and dated 7 August 2006. It reads:

> Your version of events coincided with one of the lines of investigation pursued by the police. The information you provided added to the existing material details, which were not known previously. This enabled officers from the Criminal Investigations Section of the District Police Headquarters in Będzin to undertake actions, which resulted in identifying a witness to the event and collecting the evidence that provided proof of the perpetrator's guilt and his temporary detention.
>
> With thanks for the help provided and hope for future collaboration.

KOMENDA POWIATOWA POLICJI
W
BĘDZINIE

ul.Bema 1, 41—300 Będzin, tel. (0 32) 3590280, e-mail: [illegible]

Będzin 7.08.2006 r.

Szanowny Pan
Krzysztof JACKOWSKI

Komenda Powiatowa Policji w Będzinie składa podziękowanie za udzieloną pomoc w sprawie zabójstwa Jadwigi S█████████ i Tadeusza B██████████ oraz podpalenia kamienicy w dniu 2.01.2006 r. w Będzinie przy ul. Modrzejowskiej █

Przekazana przez Pana wersja zdarzenia zgadzała się z jednym z obranych przez nas kierunków śledztwa.
Uzyskane od Pana informacje uzupełniły posiadane dane o nieznane wcześniej szczegóły.

Dzięki temu funkcjonariusze Sekcji Kryminalnej Komendy Powiatowej Policji w Będzinie przeprowadzili czynności, które dały efekt w postaci ustalenia świadka zdarzenia oraz zebrania materiału dowodowego pozwalającego na udowodnienie sprawcy winy, a także na jego tymczasowe aresztowanie.

Dziękując za udzieloną pomoc, wyrażam nadzieję na dalszą owocną współpracę.

Z wyrazami szacunku

KOMENDANT POWIATOWY POLICJI
w BĘDZINIE

ml.insp. mgr inż. Dariusz BRANDYS

Case 2: *Where to find evidence, 2001*
Location: Biedaszki Małe, village in Masuria (north-eastern Poland)
Summary:

This killing took place in the village of Biedaszki Małe in Masuria. On 20th May 2000 the police dug up the body of an elderly man, Wacław G. The head was missing, having been hacked off. The previous day around noon the man took a scythe and went to cut some nettles. When he did not come back at the usual time his wife looked for him near the railway track where they always cut nettles, but could not find him. The next day, after an anxious night, she alerted her daughter and the police in Kętrzyn, the nearest town.

The police brought a tracker dog to Biedaszki. The dog caught the scent and led them to the railway track, where in a water-filled ditch they found a sheet for gathering nettles and the man's scythe. Traces on the side of the track indicated that somebody had crossed to the other side, and not far from there a policeman noticed that the earth had been freshly dug. They started digging and found the man's headless body about half a metre under, with a hand saw next to it, most likely the tool used to cut off the head.

They called in technical experts who suggested that the murderer might have forced alcohol down the victim's throat, which would account for the high level of alcohol in the victim's blood.

Apart from the murder weapon the police had no other clues; there were no possible motives, not one single anchor point. There were no indications that Wacław G. had any enemies. A number of hypotheses were investigated, including the idea that the crime was committed by Satanists (because of the way the killing was carried out). However, none of these versions led anywhere and finally the case came to a dead end.

A year after the event the police decided to ask Krzysztof Jackowski for help. Two police officers from the CID section of the District Police Headquarters in Kętrzyn went to Człuchów.

They told the clairvoyant that the body of a middle-aged man had been found near a small village, next to a track, with the head missing. In a suitcase, in a paper bag, they brought the victim's work trousers that he had on when his body was found, with dried mud still on them. Since this item was part of the evidence, the officers could not leave Jackowski alone with it, which meant that they personally witnessed Jackowski doing a reading.

He sat down opposite one of the officers, and, in spite of feeling a little awkward initially, he shortly seemed to become absorbed in the victim.

His first impressions were that the man was walking along the road alone. Quiet, modest but happy because he seems to have been paid quite a lot of money. He then met another man, about forty. They talked and went to that man's house, an old house in the country, quite dilapidated.

After a break the clairvoyant refocused and told the police officers that he felt the two men went into that house, that there was first a drinking session and then murder and robbery. In response to questions about the murderer Jackowski told them that the man had no wife or children, and that he lived with his father, who was very lame in his right leg.

He then sensed that a fight broke out after the men got very drunk, with the host grabbing an axe and hitting the victim many times. According to Jackowski, the murderer then dragged the bloodied body to the barn nearby, took the money out of the victim's pocket, went back home and kept drinking vodka until he fell asleep. In the morning, when he woke up sober he remembered everything. He was probably in shock. He cleaned up quickly, washed the floor where the blood had splashed and dried. When things were more or less tidy he went to the barn, feeling frightened. He cut off the head, and seemed to have wanted to cut up the body and burn it in the stove, but after cutting off the head he gave up. He decided to get the body away, and that's what he did.

What followed after another break was the most important piece of information for the investigators. Jackowski felt that there was something that might provide evidence in this case, even though after a year it was unlikely there would be any traces. It seemed to him that the murderer hid the shirt he had on at the time inside the sofa bed in his room, and that had a lot of the victim's blood on it. If that shirt was still there that would prove that the murder took place there.[40]

A week later the suspect was under arrest. It was the victim's neighbour, 42-year-old Kazimierz W., a bachelor who lived with his father who was in fact lame. In their carpentry workshop traces of the victim's blood were found, and a bloodied shirt in the old sofa bed. This was the main piece of evidence against its owner.

---

[40] When describing the case in his autobiography Jackowski talks about "hearing", or feeling the instruction: "Tell them that he is over 50, never had a wife and has always lived with his elderly father, let them open the old sofa bed in his room and they will find my blood there." (Świątkowska & Jackowski, 2012, vol. I, p. 233)

In August 2001, the court in Kętrzyn had the man arrested at the request of the prosecutor's office, but the evidence was found to be insufficient and he was declared not guilty. The first "not guilty" verdict was given on 4 June 2003 but the Appeal Court in Białystok had it reviewed. The man was found not guilty again on 22 October 2004. The court did not question the DNA evidence, but it could not be established when and how the blood found its way onto the shirt.

JACKOWSKI SHOWED US THE WAY

Based on Krzysztof Janoszka's interview with Krzysztof Pieniak, retired officer from the Police District Headquarters in Kętrzyn, November 2013.

I think we need to employ all the methods that might help to solve a case so long as they are legal. I think that some of the information obtained from Jackowski can be of practical use; I don't know about all of it. We got Jackowski to help us in three cases; in one case thanks to his visions we found evidential material.

The man takes no money from the police; he never did. All he wants is confirmation in the cases where he really helped. He truly cares about documenting his work.

We were being hassled all the time: why did we go to Jackowski for help? For me, working in the police force at that time, that was normal – a personal source of information, that's all. I did not spend any official money on it. So if you have nothing it is worth trying to get help, to get some anchorage.

Where Jackowski is concerned, I need to start by saying that we had nothing, absolutely nothing to go on. Somebody had hidden a sheet with cut nettles in a culvert under the railway bank, that was all. There was no anchorage at all. Satanists, all sorts, the versions that were circulating! Just about everything was being considered. But at the end of the day we were left with nothing, and that's why we went to see Jackowski.

We gave him the dead man's clothing, and suddenly he started doing session in front of us. He took the clothing in his hands, he crumpled it; he smelled it. Then he got up and walked around the room smoking. Then he told us what he sensed. He also asked for a bit more time so that he could try to put it all on paper. In a little while he brought us four sheets torn out of a notebook, full of very detailed information.

Among other things, he said that the killing involved father and son, farmers who have cows and horses. There are traces of blood in the building where there used to be a barn. The two managed to cut off the head.

I have no idea how he could have known this. First of all, he never asked us what kind of killing was involved. All he wanted to know was what our problem was, and we said it was murder. Then he said that he wants to know the victim's first name, age, and something that had belonged to him. Nothing else.

After he gave us his version of the events we started checking out all the locals and we did establish that the victim's neighbours were a father and son, and that they had a farm and a carpentry workshop. We had already interviewed them a number of times.

We then brought in the technical people from the forensics lab and they conducted a thorough inspection of the flat at the farm and that workshop. And they did find traces of blood in the workshop and in the flat. It was not a large amount, not such that one would get when hacking off a head, because there would be a lot of splatter. But there was blood. We found it on the clothes of the suspect and in the workshop on the floor, on a rag. It turned out to be the blood of the murder victim. Before these things went to be examined we asked the suspect whether the murdered man ever visited him, whether he had perhaps cut himself on something there? But he said the murdered man had never visited and his blood could not be there. And then, when it turned out that the blood was there he spent a year under arrest, until he was pronounced innocent by the court.

We found the blood exactly where Jackowski told us it would be; that is why it says so in the letter of confirmation. There is no untruth there! Jackowski also wrote that the perpetrators tried to remove the traces, wash off the blood, but we would certainly find something.

He gave us specific information. The only thing is that he kept calling the building a barn. There was no barn there anymore because it was converted into a carpentry workshop, but everything else was accurate.

That building belonged to one of the accused, the son. He did away with the farm, opened a carpentry workshop. Blood was found in the building indicated by Jackowski.

As well as the building where we found traces of blood Jackowski also indicated the place where the victim's head was hidden. In his opinion we should look in the area of an old gravel pit; he even marked its location on a map. It turned out that there really was an old clay pit there.

However, we never found that head. We looked where the clairvoyant said, but we did not have any additional technical equipment. We just looked around and checked out any places where the earth looked disturbed, but found nothing. Anyway, by then it was a year since the murder.

But Jackowski helped us a great deal in that case. He identified the perpetrators and thanks to him we found evidence in the form of the victim's blood. Unfortunately the court pronounced them innocent because the evidence was insufficient, but in my opinion we found the guilty ones.

I have no idea why the killing took place; we did not find a motive. And Jackowski was not just talking rubbish; he gave us very specific information.

And that's how we regarded him, as an informant. When you have a problem with an investigation and data is scarce you start an operational investigation and that's what we did. In the investigation file there is a memo but it does not say that we used a clairvoyant; he was regarded as an informant.

The court asked me whether we had been given any information about the suspect and how did we know that there would be traces of blood at that very location. I said we established it during operational investigations.

Before we decided to consult Jackowski we obtained our superiors' consent.

Jackowski gives specific, concrete information that the police can use. In our case that was a great help. That is why I cannot say, as did the police spokesperson, that information from clairvoyants is unreliable. That is rubbish. I don't have a problem with that statement, but no working police officer would tell you that. In our case what Jackowski said was 100% true and that is why we wrote the letter confirming his contribution.

To start with I did not believe Jackowski had special powers and that anything would come of it. But having checked it out I can confirm that such an approach makes sense.

In reports from various investigations you will not find the word "clairvoyant". If it is not officially recorded then you can say that such a person does not in fact help the police ... The only trace in the operation is the use of a certain source of information. But Jackowski has many documents confirming and thanking him for his help.

KOMENDA POWIATOWA POLICJI
w Kętrzynie woj. warmińsko-mazurskie

04 Ldz.
Kr-I-   /37/2001

Kętrzyn 08.08.2001 r.

Pan

Krzysztof Jackowski

ul.

C Z Ł U C H Ó W

        Dziękuję Panu za udzieloną
pomoc w ustaleniu sprawcy zabójstwa Wacława G▓▓▓ zaistniałego
w dniu 20 maja 200 r. w miejscowości Biedaszki Małe, gm. Kętrzyn.
Na podstawie podanych przez Pana faktów - przeprowadzonej wizji
ustalono osobę podejrzaną o popełnienie tego zabójstwa. We wskaza-
nym przez Pana miejscu zabójstwa oraz odzieży podejrzanego zabez-
pieczono krew ustalając na podstawie przeprowadzonych badań DNA
że jest to krew zamordowanego Wacława G▓▓▓. W dniu dzisiejszym
zatrzymanemu sprawcy przedstawiono zarzut o dokonanie zabójstwa
Wacława G▓▓▓ i wystąpiono do Sądu Rejonowego w Kętrzynie o zasto-
sowanie środka zapobiegawczego w postaci tymczasowego aresztowania.
                        Z poważaniem.

NACZELNIK
Sekcji Kryminalnej
KPP w Kętrzynie

kom. Zbigniew Łomecki

Official letter of thanks confirming that Jackowski helped to establish
the identity of the killer by indicating where the victim's blood
would be found (the building and the perpetrator's clothing), which
enabled the police to secure the blood as evidence. From the District
Police Headquarters in Kętrzyn, signed by the Head of the Criminal
Investigations Section,
Chief Zbigniew Łomecki, dated 8 August 2001.

Case 3: *Tracking the murderer, 2000.*
Location: Radom, Masovian voivodship, east-central Poland.
Summary:

The letter from the police (Janoszka, 2014, p. 298) refers to two cases in which Jackowski made a contribution. One of them involves a brutal murder of four members of a family (Siennica, January 1996), where the version of the events provided by Jackowski "was totally correct in relation to the event which took place", but unfortunately the perpetrators were never found.

However, the second case is significant in highlighting Jackowski's clairvoyant "tracking" ability. The letter confirms that Jackowski provided the police with the precise location (the town, the street, the building and apartment) where the wanted murderer was hiding. The town was Koszalin, near the Baltic coast; the building was an old, dilapidated apartment block. To quote the relevant passage from the official letter issued by the Voivodship Police Headquarters in Radom dated 28 September 2000 and signed by the Chief Inspector:

> At this point I would like to express my sincere thanks to you for indicating the precise location of a wanted dangerous criminal who was in hiding in September of last year. The information you provided, including precise identification of the street and the building, made it possible to apprehend him.

When interviewed about Jackowski, Professor Ryszard Jaworski, who heads the Chair of Criminology at the University of Wrocław, draws attention to the above document as a factual piece of evidence. Jaworski had already encountered the results of Jackowski's "readings" in the early 1990s, at the beginning of the latter's career, over a case that involved successful recovery of a large amount of stolen cash. (Janoszka, 2014, p. 124)

Case 4: *Tracking the victim, 1993.*
Location: Zambrów, northeastern Poland.
Summary:

This account is based on an interview with Andrzej Jażdżewski, police superintendent in Jackowski's home town, who in the 1990s provided the main link between Jackowski and the various police forces seeking his help (Szczesiak, 2000, pp. 128-9). Police officers from Zambrów and Łomża arranged to see Jackowski to get information about the murder of the head of the local tax office. They gave him a notebook in a black cover and no other objects or information. They sat next to Jackowski who for a long while kept moving the notebook in front of his forehead. At one point he started talking: the owner of the notebook is dead; he was murdered; he was an office worker, aged 40 plus. He was attacked in the morning in front of his garage, as soon as he opened it. Jackowski also added that after the killers left, a woman turned up, known to the victim. Police were amazed, because that was exactly what happened, including that the woman was a bookkeeper at the same tax office and usually got a lift from the victim. Jackowski also said that in the body of the victim there was an elongated piece of metal between the ribs, above the kidney (this was confirmed, the killer's knife broke and a piece stayed in the body, which was revealed by the post mortem). The clairvoyant also described the appearance of the killers, and said there were two of them. That was all, but the police took him to the victim's grave in the hope that this might reveal more. Nothing happened, but then they took him, as an experiment, to show him the place where the crime took place. They started from the main square and Jackowski walked to the right place, into the gate between old blocks and found the right garage. It turned out that the route Jackowski took was the route usually taken by the victim.

Case 5: *Spur of the moment suicide, 2008.*
Location: Lanckorona, southern Poland.
Summary:

Jackowski was consulted by the family of a missing post office manager a few days after she suddenly disappeared. An inspector from the head office arrived unexpectedly at the post office and asked to see the accounts; the manager told him that she had left the keys to her office at home and would pop back for them, since she lived nearby. She was in her 40s, well known and liked. When she did not come back after a few hours the police were called in but the search was in vain, and a few days later the family contacted Jackowski and took to him her personal belongings. He felt she was dead, and saw her body in a lying position, around her neck a dark strap that seemed attached to a dead tree branch on an embankment. He drew a map that was faxed to Lanckorona and the next day she was found at that spot, where she hanged herself on the strap of her handbag that she hooked over the branch. Later it was found that some funds had been misappropriated from the post office.

Jackowski felt that at the time she was very frightened yet determined, something that is likely but cannot be confirmed; however, there is a letter of confirmation of the facts from the local mayor. It expresses much admiration and gratitude for the help in finding the missing person, Lucyna G. and states:

> Your instructions were amazingly correct and detailed. Without them the body might not have been found, or found in some distant future. Your instructions saved the uniformed services and others who took part in the search much effort, as well as pain and uncertainty for the family of the missing woman.

Wójt
Zofia Oszacka

Lanckorona,dnia 2008-06-12

Pan
Krzysztof Jackowski
ul. ███████ ██
77-300 Człuchów

Wielce Szanowny Panie,

    Wójt Gminy oraz Gminny Zespół Zarządzania Kryzysowego w Lanckoronie
w kilku symbolicznych słowach pragnie wyrazić szczere podziękowania oraz wyrazy
najwyższego uznania i szacunku w stosunku do Pana Osoby za udzieloną pomoc
w poszukiwaniach zaginionej mieszkanki Gminy Lanckorona –Lucyny Gi███

    Pana wskazania okazały się zdumiewająco bezbłędne i dokładne.
Bez tych wskazań mogłoby nie dojść do odnalezienia zwłok zaginionej lub nastąpiłoby
to w bardzo odległym czasie.

    Dzięki Pana wskazówkom zaoszczędzono trud i wysiłek służb mundurowych
i osób biorących udział w poszukiwaniach, skrócony został czas bólu i niepewności
najbliższej rodziny zaginionej.

    Pragniemy również tą drogą przekazać Panu życzenia zdrowia i sukcesów w tej
jakże szlachetnej misji pomocy ludziom.

           Z wyrazami najwyższego szacunku
           i poważaniem

           Zofia Oszacka

Case 6: *A missing blind person, 1999.*
Location: Karlino, western Pomerania.
Summary:

The police turned to Jackowski in the case of a man who went missing on 17 December 1998 in Karlino. Jackowski had a strange feeling that he could not see even when he focused, only had an understanding of what he should see. He sensed a narrow river, and a man walking along the bank, not noticing a root sticking out, stumbling, falling into the river and drowning. Then the body floated about 3 km away and got caught on a branch leaning in. Jackowski drew a map, which enabled the police to find the body. Until he was given official confirmation he did not know that the man who had drowned was blind.

The letter from the chief of police in Karlino confirms the use of Jackowski's services, that his sketch and description of the location of the body are part of the operational records (giving their number), and adds that they successfully used a dog to investigate the area indicated on the sketch.

Case 7: *Two bodies instead of one, 2001.*
Location: Zabrze, Silesia, southern Poland.
Summary:

A 14-year-old boy disappeared there towards the end of winter 2001, and his uncle (who lived somewhere else) came to Jackowski for help. The boy had been missing for two days. All Jackowski knew was the boy's name and that he went missing in Zabrze. Jackowski used a photo of the boy to focus; he felt that the boy was under water, but not alone: there was another body next to him. He had the impression of two small ponds and the name "biskup". He looked at a map of Zabrze that showed the district of Biskupice, where there were two ponds next to each other. He marked on the map where he felt there were two bodies.

A few weeks later a police officer from Zabrze telephoned with the information that they found the missing boy's body where Jackowski said it would be, as well as the body of his friend. They probably went onto thin ice. To start with, the police ignored the information and the map because, based on other information, they assumed that the boy was alive and would return home. The body was found by a passer-by but the police honourably provided official confirmation, in the form of a letter from the Police Headquarters in Zabrze, of the fact that the information provided by Jackowski regarding two missing boys from Zabrze-Biskupice was accurate, that he had sent them a map showing the location of the pond where the bodies were, and that was where they were found.

Case 8: *Missing person: from intuition to calculation, 2005.*
Location: Turek, central Poland.
Summary:

In April 2005 the family of an elderly woman asked Jackowski to help find their relative who went missing, was diabetic and would die without medication. They supplied him with a photo and clothes, and suddenly he sensed that she was dead. She had been walking along a winding narrow river, fell in and drowned. Jackowski thought this strange because the river was as narrow as a ditch, so it seemed unlikely that she could have drowned there.

He also had the feeling that he had to calculate the distance from a little concrete bridge close to the road. He drew a detailed map where he marked all these elements, the winding river and various branchings from the path along which the woman had been walking. While he was drawing he saw next to the woman's body, close to the bank, a cement bollard. The family would not accept this version, that the old woman would have walked so far, and Jackowski himself doubted his vision. However, the decision was made to search the area he indicated, 4 km from the bridge, and they did find an overturned old bollard, but no body, yet the water was too shallow for them to have missed it.

But when they looked again they found the woman's body in the water: next to the concrete bollard beavers had built a dam and the water rose in that particular place to about 2m. The police confirmed in an official letter that the body was found where the clairvoyant claimed it was, quoting the case number, while Janusz Szalewski from the Regional Prosecutor's Office in Turek made a statement to the local newspaper ("Przegląd Koniński" April 2005, No. 15):

> We use scientific methods, but we pursue all clues. We did so in this case. I have to admit I was shocked when we found the body in the precise location indicated by the clairvoyant. He drew the map of the area as if he'd been there himself. The branching of the paths, the little bridge, even this thicket. We were looking for the missing woman somewhere completely different, and if it hadn't been for this map we would not have gone there at all.

Case 9: *The body that wanted to be found, 2007.*
Location: Węgorzewo, Masuria, northeastern Poland.
Summary:

Nineteen people drowned when a sudden, powerful storm hit the lake district where people were sailing. All the bodies were located except that of Józef Lipina. His son, who had been in the boat with his father but survived, was determined to find his father's body, and took his father's recently worn clothes and a photograph to Jackowski. According to Jackowski's account, he felt strange, as if there were someone with him in the room. He took a shirt out of the bag with the clothing and put it on, as if something had made him do it. He looked in the mirror, held the other clothing and suddenly knew where the body was, which enabled him to draw a map with lots of details. The police thought it was unlikely that the body was at the location drawn by Jackowski, since it was 4 km from where the man had drowned. However, they checked it out anyway and found the man's body.

The events are confirmed by a number of documents. There is a letter from the Regional Police Headquarters, dated 10 October 2007, thanking Jackowski for his help in finding the body of Józef L., the last one to be found of the victims of the deadly squall that hit the Masurian lakes on 21 August 2007. It enabled the police to end the search, which had gone on continuously using much manpower and equipment, and allowed the family closure. There is a letter dated 1 October 2007 from the mayor of Ruda Śląska thanking him for his "invaluable help" in finding the body. And most touchingly, there is a letter from the family, worth quoting at length:

> We turned to you on 29 September 2007 to ask for help in finding the body of the late Józef L., who was lost during the squall in Masuria on 21 August 2007.
>
> Nearly six weeks had passed from that accident, with firemen, police, Volunteer Water Rescue Service and divers searching the lake and the surrounding area where the tragedy took place, unfortunately without success. Eventually the search was limited to twice daily patrols on the lake, and we did not know what else to do.
>
> In pain and desperation we went to you, and you did not refuse, even though you were not well (flu).
>
> You gave us a map which next day, in Masuria, turned out to be **invaluable** [bolded in the original text]. This map showed the shore of the lake with a cross marking the location of the body, immobilised,

in an enormous reed bed. We listened with great care to everything you said so as to pass the exact information to the police.

On 30 September I went with the police and others in motorboats onto the lake Łabap. About 11:30 the firemen, the police, the volunteers and I myself, we all went into the reed bed to search the area you indicated. About 14:45 one of the policemen and a fireman found the body – **exactly at the location you marked.**

Thank you for your help from the bottom of our hearts. There are no words to express what we feel. Thanks to you we found our beloved father, uncle and friend. That was a profound experience for us, that had a spiritual dimension. Thanks to you the body was recovered and we could arrange for a proper burial, which took place on 5 October 2007 at the church of Mary Mother of God in Ruda Śląska. We shall think of you every time we visit Józef's grave.

With best wishes for you and your family, we owe you a great debt of gratitude. Signed by family members.

Case 10: *Intervention by murder victim? The case of Sylvia filmed by TV crew.*

Jackowski did not think that the dead spoke to him when he started out as a clairvoyant. He thought he was just getting mental impressions of the past, but since then he has changed his mind, and the main case which caused him to do so took place in 2003. It involved an attractive young woman, aged around 30, called Sylvia. Sylvia disappeared without a trace a year earlier from Częstochowa, a city in southern Poland. The following account is taken from Jackowski's autobiography, giving his impressions:

I approached this reading like many others. I received a blouse of the missing person and a photograph showing an attractive 30-year old woman with dark hair and beautiful eyes. I only knew that her name was Sylvia, that she was 30 years old, and that she disappeared a year earlier in Częstochowa. The situation was not typical, because I was to carry out the reading facing a camera placed before me. The reason was simple, they were making a series about me called "Experiment – Clairvoyant" [Polsat, 7th episode] with myself in the main role. This case was brought to me by the producers of the programme, who were asked to do so by the police from Częstochowa.

I sat there, stared at the picture, smelled the blouse ... after a short time I sensed something:

"The woman lives alone but she has a daughter," I said tentatively. "She liked a freewheeling life. She was very scared of the man she did not live with but they were linked by some secret ..."

I increasingly got the "feel" of her. That is always the case in clairvoyance: the longer you keep reading, the more you sense the inner person, the personality. Sylvia's inner person was making me quite uneasy.

"The girl is cunning. She is blackmailing someone ... She knows about someone's death. She knows something about a murder!"

My anxiety kept growing.

"She knows about someone's death; it is a killing!" I repeated. "She is dead; she was murdered. She was murdered by two men she knew. She was in this detached house; to the side was a garden, an orchard. She quarrelled with these men; she wanted something from them; she was murdered in that house. She was strangled ... After she was strangled she was dragged to the garage and the whole body was wrapped in plastic sheeting."

I suddenly stopped the reading, thinking that the story is too sensational, that perhaps it is not what I am seeing but my imagination at work.

Apart from the camera facing me in the room there were Ania Janusz, the director of the series, and Paweł Kasprzak, cameraman and sound mixer all in one. I looked at them uncertainly, as if to ask if what I said made sense, but they only looked at me blankly.

After a while I looked at the photo again.

"Yes, yes, she was murdered" I said but with less conviction. "But it is strange, where her body is ... There is another body there, only I don't know if it is a woman or a man, but not in that house ... It is somewhere outside. It is some sort of dumping area.

(Świątkowska & Jackowski, 2012, vol. I, pp.12-17)

The director told him that his story was better than any of Hitchcock's but was unlikely to make sense; they had little information from the police but whatever they knew pointed to the woman being alive and having gone abroad with a German boyfriend; that she really had a little daughter that she left with her mother. When the police officers gave things to the crew they only said that since the divorce she has had a number of rich men friends and led a dissolute life.

Jackowski was cross with himself that evening: why did he come up with that nonsense? At 5 pm the next day he went back to the hotel to face the camera, with Ania and Paweł. Ania told him they would not continue with Sylvia's case and it would not be included in the series because of his obvious mistake. She then gave him a photo and an object belonging to a young man, the next case. He tried to concentrate but was getting nowhere. All the time he had Sylvia on his mind and the question: "Why did I make a mistake? Why did I feel it so strongly?"

He decided to go back to Sylvia's case and had an argument with the director who did not want to waste time on material that would not be included in the series. But he insisted, spent some 15 minutes staring at the photo, felt her cunning, her free and easy attitude again but could not say anything. Then suddenly he heard two sentences and said them aloud to the camera:

I was brought up by Granny Freddy! [feminine form in Polish] *I lived through Bogdan's death!*

He was told off for wasting time and got on with another case. But later, when the crew returned Sylvia's things to her mother, who also did not believe Sylvia was dead but wanted to see the recording, they learnt that the two items of information were true: as a child Sylvia had spent a great deal of time with her granny whose name was Freddy (Fredzia), and with her father, Bogdan, who was divorced from her mother and with whom Sylvia kept in touch, and had died two years before her disappearance.

A month later the TV people got in touch again and told him that Sylvia had been murdered. The police, while investigating a different case, that of a missing man, found two suspects who admitted to the murder and to getting rid of the body. Sylvia was the wife of one of the suspects. She knew about the murder of the other man, tried to blackmail her husband and ended up wrapped in plastic foil as well.

What stunned Jackowski were the two sentences that he said to the camera: the two details that related to Sylvia, that "proof of identity" of the victim, rather than details about her death. As he put it, this was not a dead memory; this was in the here and now. We will look at the implications of this case in a wider context later, but the main problem it poses for the materialist worldview is pinpointed by the operational officer in charge of the case:

INTERVIEW WITH THE OPERATIONAL OFFICER BY IGOR T. MIECIK

(Newsweek, 19.08.2009)

The case of a missing person that I was in charge of interested the makers of the TV series "Experiment – clairvoyant", with Jackowski as its chief character. We were looking for the missing Sylvia S. She supported herself with casual jobs and, to put it politely, she was not averse to male company. She would often travel abroad to work. We hypothesised that she went to Germany with one of her lovers. The programme makers let us have a cassette with the recording of Jackowski's "vision".

Two months later, colleagues from Częstochowa, working on a totally different case, arrested Sylvia's murderers, her ex-husband and his brother. They did kill her, because she knew about a murder they had committed earlier. Bodies of the two victims were found in the same place, a rubbish tip in Brzeziny. Sylvia's body was wrapped in foil.

The officer adds: Jackowski claimed that he was transmitting what Sylvia said: "I was brought up by Granny Freddy; I lived through Bogdan's death". Just so that we're clear, he claimed that he had been spoken to by a person from beyond the grave. The body was supposed to provide facts unconnected with the investigation so as to improve its credibility in the eyes of the living. I'm sorry, for me that's just too much. But the information about Freddy and Bogdan was true; it was confirmed later by Sylvia's mother.

Some other confirmed cases

There are many more well documented cases where Jackowski provided vital details that helped the police to establish the circumstances of a person's disappearance, find perpetrators and discover motivations, from the 1990s until the present day. In one case a group of five young people, three of them teenage girls who left home saying they were going for a pizza, did not return. Both the families and the police were convinced that they had run off as rebellious teenagers sometimes do, but, as the search kept coming up with dead ends, one of the mothers approached Jackowski. After holding the photos of the girls, the clairvoyant felt that they were dead, and that the boy who drove the car chose a less frequented route so as to avoid being stopped by the police and the car ended up in the river. The police initially did not want to follow this unexpected lead, but, after the chair of the local council intervened, a sonar was employed at that spot and showed a large object at the bottom of the river. That was the car, and the bodies of five young people were in it. In a letter of thanks to all involved in the search, the chair of the local council also thanks Krzysztof Jackowski for providing the map, which largely contributed to finding the missing people (Janoszka, unpublished documentation, Tryńcza, 2017).

In his autobiography, Jackowski reports a case that did not involve working with the police but perhaps goes further than most in its lack of glamour and sophistication in much of his clairvoyance work. On this occasion, in February 2007, Jackowski was asked to locate the missing village elder from a village in Mazovia. Since his first vision was vague, apart from the feeling that the man was dead, and a search of the general area he indicated did not produce results, he was asked to visit it himself. He spent the day searching the forest with the others, following various clues provided by the locals, and by the afternoon felt totally discouraged and embarrassed, until a friend reminded him that running around and searching was not what he would normally do. So he sat down in the missing man's room, picked up a shoe, and then got the message "look for me next to the potato stack". The family told him that potatoes were kept in the barn; they all rushed out there, and when they disturbed a thick haystack next to the potatoes they disturbed the body and were nearly overcome with the odour of decomposition. The man's widow started cursing someone and it emerged that she blamed their neighbour, an alcoholic, who organised secret drinking sessions even though he knew the husband had health problems and was not allowed to drink alcohol. It was in fact the neighbour who hid the body after the man collapsed, as was later established by the police investigation (Świątkowska & Jackowski, 2012, vol. II, pp.13-15).

On a less sombre or unpleasant note, there is also a letter from the year 2000 from the regional police headquarters in Człuchów, thanking Jackowski for his help in establishing the identity of the burglars who broke into a house. Jackowski's version of events, different from that envisaged by the police was fully confirmed, as was his description of the burglars, which enabled the police to apprehend them, and the police hope for future collaboration. There are letters from grateful families thanking him for help in locating relatives with dementia and other problems, who have wondered off, got lost but were found alive. He finds missing objects, art objects of great sentimental value stolen from well known people, machinery and money, all confirmed by letters from relatives and grateful owners. There is also the case of finding a missing dog, working from a photograph, when the name of the street "Kwiatowa" comes into his mind. The owner (in another town, in Bydgoszcz) went knocking on all doors along the street and someone had taken the dog in (Świątkowska & Jackowski, 2012, vol. 2, pp. 128-9).

Jackowski's clairvoyance: the process

In all these cases we find varying volume of information provided, and, at least in some cases, we get clues as to the routes by which it is obtained. What they have in common is the focus on the intent; on reaching a target that can be quite complex, yet the starting point is a photo, sometimes not even a name, and a personal item. Retracing in detail the steps of a missing person, a murder victim or a criminal may be astounding enough, but in the case of the double murder and arson Jackowski homes in on the motive, and that involves describing a location that no longer exists and relationships that reach years into the past; he then suggests a future course of action that may not qualify as precognition, but is the kind of prediction that sounds very much like Smith's "truncated causal chain" involved in precognition: if the police question the murderer's girlfriend, she will break – which is in fact what happens. The truncated part is the clairvoyant "knowing" what the girl knows and her likely response. The outcome: the target is exactly what the police need, a route to the identity of the murderer, initially through motive. Yet in the case of the murder in Biedaszki, the motive remains unclear, and it may never have been clear to the murderer in a drunken state; what is important is evidence. Jackowski knows that evidence is a problem after so much time has passed, but what, apart from his intention to find it, could have led him to the shirt hidden in the sofa? If the memory of it had been in the mind of the perpetrator he surely would have got rid of it. This brings to mind the comments by many of the sitters in the mediumistic séances of Mrs

Piper mentioned earlier: the impression that she digs out information buried somewhere in the recesses of their minds but not present in their conscious memory (Gauld, 2022).

When we examine the clairvoyant process in Jackowski's cases, it is very much as described by Joe McMoneagle, starting with the initial "taste", an intuitive clue with unknown (truncated) origin, which provides possibilities for combining intuitions with rational calculation. For example, when he is looking for two missing boys (Case 7), his intuition tells him that they are dead, that there are two ponds, and the name "biskup" is somehow involved. He then does some research using a map but eventually relies on intuition again to pinpoint the bodies. A similar situation arises when he locates a missing dog from a photograph brought by an elderly lady from Bydgoszcz, desperate to recover her companion (Świątkowska & Jackowski, 2012, vol 2 p. 128-130). He did not think he could do it, assuming that the information source of his clairvoyance had to be human, but he focused as he would for a human being and the "taste" was that the dog was alive. When the name "Kwiatowa" jumped into his mind he looked up a map of Bydgoszcz on his computer and found Kwiatowa Street at the other end of town from where the lady lived. In Case 8, Jackowski senses death but has no understanding and no emotional clues; he draws a detailed map with a winding river, then has to calculate the distance from the road to the little bridge that he envisaged, and then he intuitively pinpoints a cement bollard next to the body. So, again as in the case of McMoneagle, the "taste" is not enough: both intuition and research are involved.

As Jackowski recounts it, after the first "taste" there is a feeling of doubt, that he is only imagining things. He then tries to put the case to one side until the "flashes" start coming spontaneously; he then begins to get the atmosphere of the event. When he has an image in mind he writes down what he senses and draws a map. Usually it is more than a vague idea of water, a forest or perhaps a road; it will contain very specific elements that can be verified before the actual search begins.

The way that the information arrives also varies. It can be a bird's eye view, as in seeing a dead little girl, "I saw her from above. She was lying there curled up. I could see her back. Why did I see her like that? Was she also perceiving herself from a bird's eye view at that moment?" (Janoszka, 2018, p.29) This is the question that Jackowski asks again and again, in dozens of cases of drownings, where nobody knows the body's location and position.

We then come to the question of psychometry. Jackowski describes the photos, the smelling and the handling of personal belongings as his "technology" (Świątkowska & Jackowski, 2012, vol 2 p. 130), and clearly he relies on the ritual. This is a very personal aspect of clairvoyance since remote viewers, dowsers and indeed mediums have quite different procedures that do not involve psychometry. On the other hand, we do not know by what channels the information arrives in truncated chains, and the senses of smell and touch seem to be very significant for Jackowski: something particularly apparent in the case where he puts on the drowned man's dirty shirt and feels his presence.

There are many clairvoyants with impressive track records (Ingo Swann, Pat Price, Eileen Garrett, or the Pole, Rev. Father Klimuszko[41], are some that spring to mind). However, the most relevant detailed comparative material in which to place Jackowski's cases in terms of reliable reporting and contrasting yet convergent targets and attitudes is provided here by two psychic virtuosi, Joe McMoneagle and Stefan Ossowiecki.

Joe McMoneagle.

Background.
Joe McMoneagle (1946-), a distinguished American Army officer, now retired, has been described as "the best Operational Remote Viewer in the history of the U.S. Army's Special Project – Star Gate" (McMoneagle, 2002, front page). He was selected for the remote viewing project by the army because he was one of the small group of people who kept surviving the most dangerous situations against all odds in various ways, somehow "knowing" when something was about to happen in a particular location, to the point when others would mimic his actions in the field.

After graduating from high school, McMoneagle joined the US Army. In 1978 he took part in a trial of psychic ability carried out on

---

[41] Father Klimuszko (1906-1980), clairvoyant and healer. He was famous in Poland, is known to have helped in police investigations, and had taken part in a number of tests involving "readings", i.e., giving information about subjects of photographs "... during that process there appears other information linked to that person – his home, those close to him and all the events of their future" (Klimuszko, 1989, p.61). These are undoubtedly beyond the information content of a photograph. As is the case with many other psychics, all records are informal and fragmentary.

behalf of the Army by Russell Targ and Harold Puthoff at the Stanford Research Institute. He was one of six people selected for the project of remote viewing (generally now known as Star Gate), and this was the beginning of his career as a 'remote viewer' in the military, working on operational requests from various bodies, including CIA, FBI, Army Intelligence and a number of other agencies. He retired from his career in the army after 13 years, with the Legion of Merit Award for distinguished military service. (McMoneagle, 2006) His task as a remote viewer in the Star Gate programme was to locate and describe military and other facilities using geographical coordinates as targets, and to provide detailed descriptions of devices kept inside such facilities. The case described below is probably his most famous exploit and provides a detailed account of the process.

The case of the Typhoon Submarine: seeing the present and the future

There are many accurate accounts of the viewing of the Typhoon submarine, probably the best known, most detailed and perhaps the most astounding case of remote viewing. The one given here is based on that by Paul Smith, another famous remote viewer, a military "outsider" who later became an "insider" (Smith, 2015, pp. 45-63):

> The story of the remote viewing of the Typhoon is not hearsay. It is not just another old "war story" that my fellow Star Gate remote viewers and I expect you to believe just on our say-so. The provenance (the chain of custody) for this information is impeccable. Copies of nearly all the original documents that still exist became available when the CIA publicly released the Star Gate project's archives in 2004. Until then they had been in the protective custody of the CIA. The account I have given in this book of the remote viewing of the *Typhoon* is authentic, taken from the actual records and not from anyone's faulty memory."
>
> There were 10 remote viewing sessions over 2 months in the autumn of 1979. They were aimed at discovering what was happening inside the building at Shipyard 402 on the White Sea in what was then the Soviet Union.
>
> The remote viewers were Joe McMoneagle and Hartleigh Trent. They reported that inside the building the Russians were building submarines. This was regarded as impossible, because the building had no access to water, while the submarine described by Joe was

totally unlike any known submarines: twice the size of anything that existed, built against the principles of naval architecture, with missile tubes in the "wrong" place. The National Security Council dismissed the data as fantasy.

However, soon after, an enormous canal was excavated between the building and the water, and almost 11 months after the remote viewing sessions the first Typhoon super submarine, of the new design precisely as described by Joe McMoneagle, was photographed in the new canal alongside the building on 28 September 1980. In the words of Paul Smith:

"At the time, I was serving as the strategic intelligence officer for the Special Forces command in Germany and had not yet even so much as heard the term "remote viewing." It was my job to review ... the latest top-secret intelligence obtained by the Special Security Office in Munich. I still recall the almost panicked tone of the intelligence cables and briefs I read and passed on to the colonel. The Soviets had outmaneuvered the Western intelligence services, taking them completely by surprise, and both sides knew it."

In this case we also learn about the process of remote viewing, from Joe McMoneagle himself (McMoneagle, 2006, p. 124). His first target was a set of geographic coordinates from which he was able to describe the location and the facility. He "saw" the right place, a cold wasteland with ice, rocks, a very large industrial building and a harbour and sea with ice caps in the distance. Next he was given a photograph of a large building of industrial type, near a large body of water, with general materials stacked outside, located somewhere in Russia (it later turned out to be Severodvinsk on the White Sea (p. 121). As he describes it: "Spending a considerable amount of time relaxing and trying to empty my mind, I imagined myself drifting down and slowly passing through the shed-like roof to the inside of the structure. ... I felt as though I was hovering inside a building that was the size of two and a half to three shopping centers, all under one roof. I had completely misconstrued the size of the building ... [here McMoneagle gives a detailed description of the inside, of giant bays between walls, scaffolding, interlocking steel pipes, cylinders being welded...] ... I felt as though I were standing inside the building and able to actually see vividly what was going on. This rarely occurs in remote viewing, but for some reason it was happening on this target ... "My vision of the target was *so precise that it almost seemed unreal.* ... I had an overwhelming sense that this was a submarine, a really big one, with twin hulls".

The case of the kidnapped general

This ability to focus extends to pinpointing the location of a kidnapped general and being aware of his thoughts. Brigadier General James Dozier, deputy chief of staff at NATO headquarters in Italy in Verona had been abducted in December 1981 by members of the Italian Red Brigade. Three remote viewers, including Joe, were charged with trying to locate him. They were given a picture of Dozier; initially they were not totally accurate about the course of the kidnapping, but all gave similar accounts. They targeted the general over a number of days and had similar impressions: "We all reported him alive and having his eyes and mouth taped shut, with a set of earphones taped over his ears, as if he were being forced to listen to music he didn't like."

A later, very successful session by McMoneagle started "... with an almost perfect image of a coastline the right-hand side of Italy towards the north". It was followed by vivid images, which felt as if he was floating over the area, able to see what he wanted to see. He seemed to be following in the footsteps of the kidnappers:

"I suddenly found myself hovering directly over a fairly large town not far from the coast and just south and southeast of a very large mountain range. I moved closer to the ground and began to pick out roadways and buildings. I followed the roads and eventually found myself near a small central plaza, across from some kind of a fountain, and picked up the smells of a butcher shop, and the faint hint of a place where they did some kind of tanning or worked with hides. I got an image of a very large apartment building and settled in on the second floor. I came out of the session knowing that I could pretty much replicate the images and streets that I had seen." McMoneagle produced a regional map that was specific enough to identify the city as Padua. He then sketched a rough street map, pointing out the location of the apartment house where the kidnapped general was being held on the second floor.

General Dozier was released unharmed from an apartment in Padua after 42 days (not on the basis of the information provided by remote viewers, which was not used). However, the General judged their viewing accurate, especially stunning in "thought-content", the personal aspect: "information in our reports had originated within his own thoughts while he was being held – blindfolded, tape across his mouth, being forced to listen to hard rock, heavy-metal music through headsets ... (McMoneagle, 2006 pp. 116-120).

McMoneagle also successfully finds missing persons and on at least two occasions accurately locates dead bodies, very much like Jackowski.

This is something which was done spectacularly on one occasion by Stefan Ossowiecki, although he is more famous for other things.

Stefan Ossowiecki (1877 – 1944)

Background

Stefan Ossowiecki became famous as a clairvoyant during the 1920s and 1930s, achieving international fame through the experiments carried out with him by such renowned researchers as Gustave Geley and Charles Richet, and published contemporaneously in "Revue Metapsychique", the journal of Institut Métapsychique International. However, Ossowiecki was never a professional psychic, and by the time he became well known he was already a man in his 40s, with a turbulent life story behind him. He came from a wealthy family of a Polish industrialist settled in Russia, and was heading the family business when the Soviet Revolution upended his life. He came to Poland in 1918 and became active as a businessman again, but it is his "career" as a psychic that really took off at this point, working with a very active group of psychical researchers from Poland and abroad. He never used his psychic abilities for financial gain or personal betterment, and put himself at the disposal of researchers.

Most of the experiments with Ossowiecki involved concealed (usually in sealed envelopes) writing or drawing, occasionally photos and packages with various objects. Sometimes the description of the wrappings and their history appears even more impressive than the successful identification of the target (as when the clairvoyant recounts the history of the box containing the target, and describes accurately where and who bought the cotton wool in which it was wrapped) (Barrington et al, 2005, pp. 71-72). At the International Congress of Psychical Research in Warsaw in September 1923 a high point in the history of psychical research was reached when the then SPR's Research Officer Eric Dingwall, who had prepared the target, an intricately wrapped drawing and writing, confirmed that the package had not been opened and drew it on the blackboard next to the drawing previously made by Ossowiecki. It was a perfect match (Dingwall, 1924; Barrington et al., pp. 62-64).

Alongside the experimental evidence, there are also many real-life cases corroborated in detail by witnesses. They involved locating missing objects or persons with the aid of psychometry, i.e., handling an object associated with the target. Ossowiecki was also responsible for a unique and almost accidental case of pure clairvoyance, when in 1935, he described accurately the contents of a package, which were unknown to anyone living. The package was mislaid and in the meantime the person who created it had died 10 years before the experiment took place without revealing its contents to anyone (Barrington et al., 2005, pp. 80-84; Semczuk, 2014).

A quite distressing case, where the nature of the target was known but its location was obscured by the presence of some 700 similar targets in its proximity, involved the identification of a corpse in a mass grave. Again, the information required was not known to anyone living.

A body in a mass grave

The account, which follows, is confirmed by Ossowiecki's widow, who described her late husband's experience.

Letter to Zofia Ossowiecka from Jerzy Olewiński, dated 27th August 1946.

... My brother, Ensign Janusz Olewiński, was killed during a cavalry charge in the locality of Palmiry near Warsaw, on 22nd September 1939... After being exhumed from the battlefield his body was put into a collective grave of about 700 Polish cavalry soldiers in the parochial cemetery of Kiełpin, district of Łomianki near Warsaw[42] ... I intended to transfer his remains to our family vault in Radom ... and tried therefore to locate the approximate place where his body lay in the over 200m long grave ... the task seemed hopeless ... I therefore contacted and visited, together with my mother, Engineer Stefan Ossowiecki to whom I brought a photograph and a letter written by my brother.

After examining both, Mr. Ossowiecki drew a detailed sketch of the cemetery and the grave, marking the spot where my brother lay. He further defined the cause of my brother's death, a heavy wound on the right side of the abdomen and groin. He also stated that he had died unattended after an hour in great pain. The sketch contained details of which we were unaware (for example, the belfry).

---

[42] More than 700 soldiers died in the battle of Łomianki (September 1939) in which Janusz Olewiński was killed, and some 8000 were wounded. It is impossible to establish the chronology of burials (many bodies were originally placed in ditches by the roadside), but the military section of the cemetery in Kiełpin was enlarged very quickly and now holds some 2300 bodies, only a fraction of which have been identified.

On our entreaties, Mr. Ossowiecki attended the exhumation in September 1940. Before the digging began we left him alone, at his request. After walking up and down the burial ground several times, Mr. Ossowiecki stopped and said that was the spot where my brother lay (it corresponded to the one marked on the sketch) and that the corpses lay in great disorder in several layers.

Upon this the workers began the digging, supervised by Mr. Ossowiecki. After setting several bodies aside he told us the next one would be the one of my brother and asked for it to be taken out of the grave. After it had been washed, my mother, sister and I recognized the body by the stature, military rank, personal garments and gold crowned tooth. The doctor attending the exhumation found the wound to the right part of the abdomen and groin. The clenched fingers proved that my brother had died in great pain ... (Barrington, 2005 p. 116.)

In the original letter there are two comments not included in the previous versions:

"The Germans denied the permission to move the body, so I interred my brother again and marked the spot. Only after the war did I transfer his remains to the family vault.

A few weeks after the experiment, Mr. Ossowiecki told me that while walking along the grave in Kiełpin he had clearly seen my brother's ethereal form."

Jerzy Olewiński

Since the publication of the book by Barrington et al., some unpublished notes came to light which Ossowiecki's widow, Zofia, was making for a programme about her husband. This account is not first hand and not corroborated, but it does come from someone who did her best to preserve Ossowiecki's legacy, and make it available to researchers. In her notes Zofia talks about the difficulties faced by Ossowiecki on that occasion, and about the lost manuscript of "Immortality", the book Ossowiecki was working on at the time of his death, which contained an account of this experience. According to her, the experience was very stressful for the clairvoyant, so he tried to focus, asked for God's help and began calling the missing man in his mind. After a while, he saw in front of him what looked like a long, vertical, misty shadow, which slowly moved towards the longest of the graves, of which there were a few. He then followed the shadow, called for the people with the spades to follow him, and pointed out where they should dig, about the middle of the grave. The top layer of the soil was removed; the first bodies were those of a major and some officers, all of them in a state of disarray. From the outset, Ossowiecki stated that the body of the cadet would be found deeper, and that was what happened. When the ninth body was brought up, he called out, without looking, that that was Janusz Olewiński.

And, finally, a case of viewing very distant past.

The ancient settlement of Biskupin

During 1936-1942 Professor Stanisław Poniatowski, an ethnologist, carried out a series of "archaeological" experiments with Ossowiecki. Poniatowski was looking for information about prehistoric cultures, and believed that Ossowiecki could supply it clairvoyantly, using psychometry to "connect" to specific cultures in the past, very much as he did when he "connected" through the objects he was given to hold with their owners and their circumstances. For a variety of reasons (one of them the probable misidentification of the psychometric objects by the archaeologist), the 33 experiments held under carefully controlled conditions and witnessed by a number of university professors gave very mixed results[43]. However, this experiment, in 1937, resulted in a remarkably precise description of a distant location that was still to be fully excavated and therefore contained information unknown to anyone. The location was the settlement of Biskupin, in north-central Poland, discovered in 1933, now known to date from the 8th century. Excavations started in 1934.

Poniatowski was the only person who knew that the piece of ceramic that served as the psychometric object came from Biskupin and, since very little of the area had been excavated, Ossowiecki's description seems to have been based purely on clairvoyance. He described people and animals, of greatest interest to Poniatowski, but it is the nature and environment of the settlement for which there is reliable verification.

Excerpts from Ossowiecki's narrative:

> "Valleys ... enormous areas under water. Rows of wooden single-storey houses, one line separated from the next one by some thirty, forty, up to fifty steps ... The impression as if there was a whole city, a small town built on such stilts ... (...) I am losing it now ... water ... I see these parallel planks, stretching far ... trees cut down, rough, all

---

[43] An account of selected experiments, with a commentary by Professor Jacek Woźny, edited and translated by Zofia Weaver, is to be found in the SPR's Lexcien library: *Archaeology experiments with Stefan Ossowiecki* which can be accessed here: http://www.lexscien.org/lexscien/index.jsp.

covered in moss and ... If you look down on it, it's like one enormous roof, and from a distance they are separated by these trees ... whole row of houses, in one direction, and another ... fifteen ...

A strange entrance, now I see ... and then from here it goes down and there is lots of water... there is water here as well, but further there is more and it goes... river, not a river... a lake of some sort ... such rows I see ... difficult to draw. There is a road ... and a passage to the water ... I see five, seven eight rows like that, and then it is blurred ... From the shore I see a wooden fence that stops the water flooding this whole apparatus... but it is all wood ... thin ... quite technical... And here to the right diagonally *(shows on the drawing)* these animals ... within the fencing, and then enormous forests all around ..."

Biskupin was a fortified settlement on the peninsula of Lake Biskupin. Originally it was an island, about a 100 m from the shore. Along the shores of the peninsula there was an oak-pine palisade, consisting of a number of rows, intended both as a breakwater and a defensive measure. The main defensive construction was a rampart built of wood and soil, with a gate and a wooden bridge, which linked the island to the mainland. Inside the rampart there were 106 houses arranged in 13 rows, divided by 11 parallel streets, which joined the widest and longest ring road. The tops of the houses touched each other and had similar dimensions, similar skeletal construction and similar household equipment. Ossowiecki's description of the enormous areas under water, rows of wooden houses, a town built on stilts with wooden ramparts protecting it from flooding, is thus accurate. However, the most exciting remarks came at the end of the experiment:

> ... here where the (settlement) ends, there is a lot of water and beyond the water there is yet another city, larger than this one; it does not exist anymore, but is at a distance of one kilometre, only larger, now buried ... enormous city ... Beyond the lake... The same people (in this other city) ... Now there is a forest there ... a town on land, but buried ... that lake flooded that city.

The local Lusatian settlements were not thoroughly researched until after the Second World War. Ossowiecki's statements about another, enormous city north of Biskupin were verified (obviously only to some extent) in the second half of the twentieth century, towards the end of the 1950s, when excavations 10 km north of Biskupin revealed a previously unknown settlement from the Lusatian culture, probably some three times larger than the settlement at Biskupin.

Kinds of clairvoyance, kinds of clairvoyants: what they have in common

When I started looking for "clairvoyant virtuosi" for this research, I found a lot more potential ones than those presented here. Bearing in mind that my research was restricted to only those cultures to which I have easy access, Anglo-Saxon and Polish, and to the best-documented cases, the world is probably much richer in virtuosi than the ones who have left a trail for psychical researchers to follow. Joe McMoneagle is probably right when he says that many people are potential psychics but do other things with their lives rather than devote them to clairvoyance as a profession.

There are many spectacular, spontaneous cases that involve clairvoyance, and many people have flashes of clairvoyant intuition; that is what one would expect if psi is an inseparable aspect of consciousness, a fundamental unconscious engagement with the world, rather than an anomalous ability. On the other hand, while there are many psychic claimants, practitioners of clairvoyance with a verified track record are few, and they tend not to identify themselves in terms of a concept that for much of the populace brings to mind "supernatural powers" and associations with the occult, while probably even more people regard it as nonsense. There are, of course, various sections of Anglo-Saxon society where mediumship is acknowledged, taught and practised within well-established organisations, and various organisations that practise and research remote viewing; however, that is not the case in Poland (see next chapter).

More importantly, the virtuosi of clairvoyance become virtuosi because they specialise in what they do. This may happen because their life path takes a specific direction (such as when Joe McMoneagle agreed to participate in the remote viewing programme), or because one event leads to another as in the case of Jackowski's fame spreading among the local people, or because they choose a specific course of action, such as Matthew Manning choosing to become a healer rather than researching his psychokinetic abilities. A number of mediums practise healing, testifying to a connection between various aspects of psi, and Jackowski had much success at giving medical diagnoses at the beginning of his career.

Most psychics are probably capable of a lot more than they do, but – and this is crucial – practice makes, if not perfect, then certainly above average.

According to Stefan Ossowiecki, he learnt the essential techniques for entering the right state from an old Jewish mystic, and worked on improving his knowledge. Joe McMoneagle points out that, particularly with remote viewing, he was "basically paid to do that [spending] 12-hour days for years and years just learning and perfecting" (McMoneagle, 2012). Jackowski has now been a successful clairvoyant for more than 20 years. And the virtuosi get very good at what they do most often: Joe McMoneagle learns to do remote viewing almost as routine, but has to learn to manage his out-of-body experiences, which, according to him, are a very different state, and looking for what he describes as "mental triggers" takes him months of effort. By the time he becomes involved in regular tests, Ossowiecki can read through dozens of envelopes without trying very hard.

Practice means training oneself to follow certain procedures, one of which is to induce in oneself an "intentionally simplified altered state" that enables one to seek out the target and focus on it. Remote viewers and parapsychologists are explicitly aware of this and apply techniques to facilitate such a state as, for example, in the ganzfeld conditions and relaxation techniques. Ossowiecki used to ask those present to talk among themselves rather than pay attention to him, while Jackowski, where possible, seeks environments that provide distractions. Creating a suitable environment seems to be the easiest aspect of the process to identify and recreate, while the most crucial and hardest seems to be the ability to recognise what McMoneagle calls the "taste"; this sudden "knowing" is the truncated part of the process. It is different from the usual kind of scanning that is described by Carpenter as first sight that is similar to responding to subliminal stimuli and not all that strange; however, it does strike us as strange when the clairvoyant describes a scene from a thousand years ago, as does Ossowiecki when holding a piece of ceramic from Biskupin, or a submarine which does not yet exist as does McMoneagle when given the coordinates of its location, or peers into a sofa bed miles away to find the incriminating bloodied shirt that was placed there more than a year before, as does Jackowski when given a photo and a pair of old trousers to hold. What is provided is exactly the information that is wanted.

Joe McMoneagle makes the valid point that for accurate focusing, one needs to be specific about dates and times when choosing the target (he mentions a whole series of failures at Stanford Research Institute where no time was specified and the target buildings he saw were not built until years later), and to expect bleed-through from the immediate past and the immediate future (McMoneagle, 2013, loc. 2132). Yet there may be more to accurate focusing in real life cases when the intention is very specific, such as looking for a piece of evidence or being highly emotionally motivated, as when putting on the dead man's shirt that produces certainty about the body's location.

The next stage of the process is more like the sensory processing based on physical senses. It is best to follow the maxim of remote viewers: "say what you see, not what it looks like" (for example, if a stimulus is interpreted as a swarm of bees, that conclusion precludes considering any idea that is contrary to it; but if you stop at "a confusing cloud of shapes" you remain open to broader interpretations (Carpenter, 2012, pp. 27-9)). That is why every effort is made to avoid "front loading" in remote viewing, and why Jackowski prefers not to know anything about the case before he starts working on it. He is particularly wary of highly publicised cases, since it is impossible to switch off the knowledge one already has (Świątkowska & Jackowski, vol. 2 p. 131).

However, what McMoneagle calls a "taste", that basic sensation, is followed by further focusing that now involves conscious actions, such as drawing a map and providing specific elements. So this is not a simple process where suddenly all is clear; there is interaction between the intuitive and the logical, and the conclusions are based on both interpenetrating processes, complex and prolonged, and this is one of the ways in which "professionals" take "psi processing" to a different level. In remote viewing there also might be many sessions by a number of remote viewers revisiting the target before coming up with a report. Remarkably, they tend to get much convergent accurate information.

What is also remarkable is the complexity of the channels through which the information arrives. When it is visual, there seem to be multiple axes of vision; we have the distant bird's eye view such as McMoneagle's first impression of the landscape around the building housing the submarine, or of the city of Padua where General Dozier is held, or Ossowiecki's first impressions of enormous waters around Biskupin, or a belfry near the burial field that holds the body he is locating, or Jackowski's view of the village with the characteristic church where the girl with the vital evidence is to be found. But then you get detailed views of the design or the characteristics of the target, the submarine, the identifying marks of the buried body, the features of ancient settlement, or the underwater spring next to which the drowned body is to be found in one of Jackowski's cases. It seems that the mind at large operates differently, in a way that resembles some of the near-death experience accounts, like that of a woman who in that state "saw" a plaque with the manufacturer's name under the operating table she had been on, which was later found to be there. She described it as having "multiple axes of vision, from many places at once" (Rousseau, 2011, p. 208).

Relevant information can also be "heard": when looking at a photo of the missing dog Jackowski "hears" the name Kwiatowa [adjectival form of "flower", which makes him think it refers to Kwiatowa/Flower Street]. This turns out to be correct, yet is unlikely to have come from the missing dog. As he puts it when talking about the information that seems to come from the dead, it is not so much hearing as understanding (Świątkowska & Jackowski, vol. 2, p. 56). This brings to mind an explanation of how the messages from the dead reach her, given by Feda, supposedly a young Indian girl who acted as the "control" of the famous medium Mrs Osborne Leonard:

> Well, sometimes I sees a thing that I ought to hear, but I can't hear it, so I sees it, do you see? ... And sometimes I can only hear a thing and I can't see it at all. Some sittings I just happen to be in what you would call ... the seeing vibration. And if I gets into it then it is easier to see whatever has been told me; it is easier to see it in pictures or in symbols. But another time, if I happen to get into a hearing vibration ... then it is easier to hear" (Gauld, 2022, p. 260).

This does not provide greater illumination; it just demonstrates that the channels of communication have been open for a long time and remain mysterious.

As has already been said, it seems that the most perceivable targets are emotionally significant or dramatic (Schwartz, 2014, p. 12), but this does not mean emotional involvement by the clairvoyant/remote viewer, as opposed to strongly engaged intent. Mediums can also be remarkably matter of fact about contacting the discarnates when they do it professionally (Gauld, 2022). However, in the case of Jackowski, emotional engagement seems to play a vital role. It may be that his attitude and manner of working is affected by the kinds of targets he deals with, becoming immersed in the current human distress that becomes very real to him. For him, physical contact with a photograph or personal possession seems essential, as it did for Ossowiecki, and a number of other clairvoyants have felt that handling an object belonging to someone helped to establish contact. The significance of psychometric objects is not clear, but there is one interesting semi-anecdotal account that may have some bearing on the subject. During some experiments organised by professors from Warsaw University in 1963, Father Klimuszko was given a number of photographs to comment on, which he did successfully. However, in one case he gave a "reading" that applied to the person who stole the photograph rather than the person pictured in it. The photograph showed the experimenter's daughter, but Klimuszko described a psychopathic "monster" who was causing a great deal of concern to the person caring for her. This fitted the personality and events surrounding a deeply disturbed girl, an orphan who stole the photograph and carried it on her person for two weeks (Klimuszko, 1989, p. 38). There is also the case of Ossowiecki asking for a different, more personal object when he attempts to make contact with the target person (Barrington, 2005, p. 113), while some of Jackowski's readings can involve intense physical immersion (smelling, handling). This may be yet another channel of information flow that is present to a greater degree in some individuals.

The clairvoyants discussed here are very different personalities, come from different backgrounds and cultures, but achieve success in similar tasks involving psi. They also have other things in common: they know how to shape the conditions required for success, even if they don't always work; they have their beliefs and rituals, which they have worked out over years of experience that give them confidence; they know how to calm themselves, to reduce unnecessary input and to fire but control their imagination; they have the resilience to accept failure, and the analytical judgment to hold back the "intellectual overlay" when it would interfere with the experience, but employ it in interpreting the experience.

However, if psi is operating all the time, why are there so few clairvoyants around, and why does it appear that only 1% of us are capable of making use of this innate ability, and even that 1% often gets it wrong (65% success rate being regarded as high)? Why can't more of us make use of it? Practice indeed makes a difference, but there appears to be something else that distinguishes the virtuosi. It has been suggested that most mediums had some kind of traumatic experience in their past, and this is certainly true of the virtuosi discussed here. Ossowiecki is reported to have had psychic experiences since puberty, but it seems to have been the trauma of imprisonment and being sentenced to death during the Bolshevik revolution that released what he regarded as his spiritual powers. Joe McMoneagle had a difficult, quite traumatic childhood and was probably psychic all his life; but he did not realise it and accept responsibility for it until after he went through a near-death experience at the age of 24, when he watched the efforts to resuscitate him, finding himself popping in and out of his body (McMoneagle, 2006, p. 177). Father Klimuszko's psychic development followed traumatic experiences during World War 2 when he was beaten and tortured by German soldiers. Jackowski's trauma seems to be on-going, and involves an unresolved urge to seek the meaning of life and his experiences.

So perhaps it is having an NDE, like Joe McMoneagle, or a traumatic experience like facing a death sentence for Ossowiecki, or rejecting your life like Jackowski, that is the link between these people; perhaps it somehow unbalances the usual relationship between mind and body and enables them to enter states of consciousness, which are not available to those of us who have avoided trauma; perhaps it means a degree of disengagement from the reliance on physical senses. Which brings us to back to Grosso's question mentioned earlier: if psi is universal on a small scale yet seems to work only sometimes and only for some individuals that are unusual in some way on a scale that can make a big difference, then what is it for?

8

CLAIRVOYANCE AND
LIFE AFTER DEATH

~

Research into meaningful connections vs cultural
backgrounds

So far, plenty of evidence has been quoted to show that "... the mind interacts with meanings, however we may ultimately come to understand that. And it is not simply propelled into action. It seeks them and engages them intentionally" (Carpenter, 2012, p. 87). When it comes to survival, the unresolved question is: whose mind? Much research has gone into the evidence for mediumship, reincarnation and near-death experiences, and much philosophical discussion has taken place as to their significance, but no definitive answer has been forthcoming. This chapter does not attempt to provide one, but looks at the evidence of clairvoyance in the context of motivated psi, cultural backgrounds and the possibility of adding to our ideas about what psi might be for.

As has been said earlier, mediumship is the kind of clairvoyance where the target is the discarnate person with whom the sitter wants to communicate, so the motivation comes from the sitter. Mediums claim to be able to differentiate between information from the living and from the discarnates, and there is research that supports this claim (Radin, 2018, pp. 161-2). On the other hand, since the intent also involves the medium acting on behalf of the sitters, there is the possibility of the motivated medium becoming entangled in the available unconscious content, as was observed by Rosalind Heywood when the medium took her fears for the target as fact. Jackowski also claims to know whether the target is alive when he tries to locate missing persons: according to him, this is a logical consequence of the fact that the dead do not move around much.

Research into remote viewing is concerned with clairvoyance in scientific and practical terms, identifying and describing distant or future targets. Research into mediumship is concerned with clairvoyance in relation to the possibility of contact with the dead. However, in Poland at present there seems to be no room for either kind of research at all. The popular attitude is perhaps best summed up in the reaction – to the idea of using a clairvoyant – of the policeman who interviewed Jackowski over the murder and arson case in Będzin: "I live close to a church but I am not a believer". For historical reasons, Roman Catholic religion has been and is a very powerful influence in Poland, and its teaching expressly forbids attempts to communicate with the dead, regarded as a mortal sin. This means that mediumship never took root among the Polish population at large (Mikołejko, 2019, pp. 49-69), and the Catholic religion's exclusive claim to all things spiritual is reflected in the policeman's attitude. This might account for some of the extreme reactions to the phenomena of clairvoyance in Poland, which, for some, implies a religious belief, and by some is interpreted as dabbling in the occult, necessarily fraudulent, mistaken or the result of satanic influence.

With no tradition of mediumship and mediumship research, claims such as Jackowski's claim that the dead speak to him do not fit into the available worldviews. On the other hand, with materialism as the mainstream worldview, investigating paranormal manifestations and unexplored human abilities is also viewed with suspicion as encouraging irrational superstition. Even at a time when taking a rational approach to the paranormal seemed to achieve scientific respectability and public acceptance, in the period between the two World Wars (1918-1939), the new science of metapsychics, devoted to exploring the newly discovered forces in the human psyche and their relation to biology[44], expressly

---

[44] The year 1919 saw the opening of International Metapsychics Institute (IMI) in Paris, with the physician Gustave Geley as its director and the Nobel-prize winning physiologist Charles Richet as an active researcher.

rejected any attempts at mixing psychical research with the question of survival of bodily death. At the second International Congress of Metapsychical Research at Warsaw University in 1923, a declaration was adopted to specifically register its protest against mixing psychical research with spiritism, stating that "no hypothesis can be regarded as proven, and survival of bodily death cannot be regarded as the only possible interpretation of psychic phenomena", and emphasizing that psychical research is not associated with any religious or moral doctrine (*Zagadnienia Metapsychiczne*, Jan/Feb/Mar 1924, p.15).

After World War 2, psychical research became ideologically incorrect in Poland under the materialist communist doctrine, and whatever research was carried out adopted a less contentious profile, focusing on activities such as dowsing (now called radiesthesis) and healing (now called bioenergotherapy) and generally becoming known as psychotronics, to fit in better with the natural sciences. However, when the communist system collapsed in 1989 this did not result in a resurgence of parapsychology; in a new, market-oriented environment, with the exception of a few individuals, the focus of psychotronics continued to be the provision of services.

With no strong organisations, such as the SPR in Britain or IMI in France, with ideological upheavals as well as physical destruction of archives and libraries during the war, it is not surprising that in Poland the subject as a whole has gone into decline. There is no private support for research, no grants, no university courses offering parapsychology as an academic subject, no academic journals, and obviously no survival research. The absence of academic research combined with scarcity of serious publications results in profound ignorance, additional suspicion of and hostility to the subject as a whole, and a tendency to conflate interest in parapsychology with religious belief. At the same time all kinds of esoteric claims, mostly unsubstantiated, flourish unchecked. In this respect Poland is not very different from the rest of the world, especially since the media often take a partisan interest in unusual/ sensational news, while the Polish Wikipedia, like its English-language counterparts, ensures that no mention of "unorthodox interests" (to borrow Andreas Sommer's phrase) appears in the biographies of notable Poles. Strangely enough, as one of Janoszka's interviewees points out, it

---

This provided psychical research, called metapsychics, with status and prominence and seemed to herald a new era of scientific discoveries (Brady Brower, 2010).

was easier for the police to make use of clairvoyants (sometimes through the families of the victims or missing persons) under communism, when the subject was simply unmentionable.

In this climate, it is not surprising that Jackowski's claim that the dead speak to him does not resonate; it has no worldview in which to fit, nor research tradition that could examine it rationally. Does it resonate any better with the evidence of clairvoyance and survival research gathered over the years in other countries?

Jackowski's evidence for survival

Jackowski has come to feel that he connects to the discarnates whose bodies he finds, that he focuses on their energies, the frequency of the other person's psyche, and he tries to "feel" into that person through their personal belongings. When he started out as a clairvoyant in the 1990s he used to think that what he was getting was just mental impressions of the past, but after 20 years he has come to believe that the dead continue to exist and that they provide the information (Świątkowska & Jackowski, 2012, vol. 1, p. 199). He describes it as not like seeing a film, but a kind of perception, sometimes in words but not exactly hearing, more like understanding. To him this has become the most important aspect of his work: proof of contact is what he seeks.

The way that the information arrives is a point to consider later, but to start with let us turn to a case from Jackowski's early days of clairvoyance. It is anecdotal, it has no date, but it sounds genuine and provides a good illustration of what, in a different culture, might have involved a visit to a medium and produced a similar result (Szczesiak, 2000, p. 199).

A woman came to see him with a photograph of her daughter, aged about twenty. The girl kept feeling ill, but the doctors could not provide a definite diagnosis. Jackowski thought she had leukemia and that she would die.

A while later the same woman came back: the girl did die, and the mother was desperate for help. You might say God had let her down by not answering her prayers, and she was full of doubts: was there an afterlife? Uncertain what to do, Jackowski looked again at the same photo of the girl, and got the following message: "I'm here with father, he is 27, his head does not ache anymore. He says that when you return to us he will not beat you anymore."

The clairvoyant thought he must be talking nonsense when in answer to his question the woman told him that her husband was alive, but then it turned out that the girl's father was her first husband, who died aged 27 of a brain tumour, was violent and a drunkard.

So while Jackowski's target is the girl whose fate the woman is concerned with, it is the father who provides the identifying clue, you might say as a drop-in communicator. We can deduce that the girl would have been about seven when he died, and there is a simple and genuine feel to the situation, while there is no uplifting message one would expect from the deceased in a different culture, one that cultivated mediumship. Surely not being beaten anymore would be a minimalist programme for an afterlife, yet it might be important to both father and child as part of the family relationship. This is pure speculation but perhaps Jackowski's impressions of contact with the dead tells us something about afterlife; his "communications" are all different, and do not sound like reassuring platitudes.

There is another case where Jackowski is convinced of the intervention of the discarnate victim (Świątkowska & Jackowski, 2012, vol. 2, p. 171-2). It was not documented, but it does involve the police and an investigation; however, that was not the reason why it made an impression on him. In the spring of 2011 he had a visit from two male and one female police officer from City Police Headquarters in Gniezno, in central-western Poland, about a macabre murder of an elderly woman. Her body was found in her own apartment, on the carpet, with her throat cut. It was puzzling because the woman had no enemies, nor was she rich, while the door to the apartment was locked from the inside.

It took about three hours to get a "reading", in the presence of the investigating officers. Jackowski was a little uncomfortable but managed to come up with a number of details that confirmed what the officers already knew, by the usual process of holding a piece of the victim's clothing to his forehead. They were amazed at how he could have obtained that information. The policewoman particularly insisted on trying to learn about the process, and Jackowski told her that he had good contact with the murdered woman, who in fact arrived with the police. He did not really know how to explain it, so he grabbed the piece of clothing (a blouse) again and got the message "tell her [the policewoman] about the herring marinade". He did so, feeling very silly, but not as silly as the policewoman. Shocked, she explained that while collecting fingerprints in the victim's apartment she had to examine every space. In the kitchen she found a handwritten note on the work surface next to the sink, with a recipe for Ukrainian herring marinade – that was the title on the piece of paper. With many years' experience behind her, for the policewoman this was just another job without great emotional involvement and, rather unprofessionally but being a keen cook, she copied the recipe into her notebook (the recipe turned out to be very tasty). The information sounds just like the kind of convincing trivial tidbit that is needed, a natural helpful prompt for Jackowski from someone who was there and saw what happened – if only that someone was not dead!

The situation sounds natural and real, apart from the fact that the helpful hint seems to come from a discarnate. Yet the information is present in the policewoman's mind, while Jackowski's intent is to demonstrate the presence of the victim, so this may be a manifestation of the natural human ability to dramatise and personify; to weave a story.

In the case of Sylvia quoted earlier, the identity of the intender is less diffuse. Here, nobody is really looking for the woman; the impression is that her photo and blouse are handed to Jackowski perhaps because the police do not regard the case as very urgent or important and therefore no damage would be done by the involvement of a TV channel. He is under pressure not to persevere and while he does not want to fail, he does not want to upset the TV people either. The way he is "pushed" to try again, and the statement that comes out on the second occasion, described by the policeman as the corpse supplying details unconnected with the case to establish its credibility, seems like a desperate attempt at making oneself heard. Identifying the communicator is one of the main preoccupations of sittings in mediumship, but here the claim about having been brought up by her granny and losing her father seems to have more to do with the victim wanting her fate known.

In Jackowski's cases the interactions with what might be the afterworld seem to be concerned with the here and now, with specifics, and not spirituality in general. There is the "unfinished business" in the case of Sylvia, reminiscent of the case investigated by Keen & Playfair, where the victim approached a medium; in the case of the woman who is looking for some confirmation of an afterlife, the promise from the father that there would be no more beatings has a very non-spiritual flavour, while the story of the herring marinade provides evidence of afterlife even more closely connected to down-to-earth matters.

There are many cases where Jackowski becomes aware of the location of the body even days after a current had carried it far from the scene of accident. He interprets these as evidence that information comes from an entity that continues to exist and is aware of what happened to its body, since there is no brain to register that memory. His belief seems to be based on the assumption that the target's brain is necessarily involved in the process of clairvoyant communication when the target is human, through producing a memory of the image of the body's location. However, as we have seen, the target does not have to be living, and a scene viewed from the bird's eye view need not be transmitted via another brain; as in so many cases of clairvoyance, and in some verified NDE cases, it seems to be a different kind of perception, not located in the brain.

So the fact that he locates bodies that have drifted far from where the person had drowned, in places with very specific characteristics, is not in itself evidence of survival. Viewing objects in obscure locations is what focused intent produces in all kinds of circumstances where no people are involved, alive or dead and, while Joe McMoneagle might conceivably have got the details of the submarine by telepathy from its designers, there were no living persons whose minds Ossowiecki could have tapped for an image of the settlement of Biskupin, and even the settlement inhabitants a thousand years ago would never have seen it from above. However, what may be most significant in the case of Jackowski is the intense physicality of the link he seems to establish with what might be described as the previous owner of the body, rather than how he views its location.

Since strong emotions are often involved in how Jackowski approaches his cases, it seems natural that he identifies with the people he seeks. He "feels" them and reports his impressions as if the dead were talking to him. There are sometimes puzzling aspects of these reports: when he has problems in locating the body of a missing diabetic old lady, he hears "look for me next to Piłsudski". He looks at the map of the town where she has gone missing; there is no street named after Piłsudski and no statue to him, but then he finds a bridge with that name and the body turns out to be in the bushes next to it. What makes this unusual is the assumption on the part of the "informant" that the name is meaningful; an assumption likely to be made by someone local to whom it is obvious that "Piłsudski" means the bridge (Świątkowska & Jackowski, 2021, vol. 2, p. 56-58). And then there is the extremely physical aspect of his efforts to make the connection, including the body that wanted to be found, with the powerful emotions of the family desperate to find the body (proper burial being a very important aspect of this culture), but perhaps also powerful emotion on the part of the owner of the body. Perhaps

Jackowski's account of feeling strange, as if there were someone with him in the room, and the unusual action of putting on the dead man's shirt, looking at himself in it and the sudden knowing where the body was, is another channel, that of physicality, not sufficiently explored, through which clairvoyant information arrives. Research has not given much attention to the function of the psychometric object, and clearly there are different ways of obtaining information clairvoyantly, but for Jackowski it seems to play a very significant part.

In his Skeptiko interview Joe McMoneagle makes a point that seems very relevant here:

> Well, I happen to believe, based just purely on my experience over the past 35 years anyway, that everything has a consciousness, all the way down to the subprimal level. In other words, the rock has a consciousness. It's the very reason why in this illusion we call space/time reality that a rock is a rock. It would be incapable of staying a rock if it had no consciousness for it.

It makes one wonder if such a totally panpsychic approach might explain, in a strangely logical sort of way, the significance of personal objects in psychometry: perhaps there is an imprint of the owner on what might be called the "consciousness potential" of the inanimate object that belonged to him/her, that somehow blends with the consciousness of the clairvoyant (this brings to mind Koch and Tononi's Integrated Information Theory, according to which "experience may not even be restricted to biological entities but might extend to non-evolved physical systems previously assumed to be mindless" (Koch, 2021).

Meaningful connections in traditional mediumship

Jackowski's experience is very focused on specific moments and fleeting experiences, but it is also important to consider traditional mediumship that attempts long-term relationships with the discarnates, without any traumatic events, if we are trying to obtain a bigger picture.

Over recent decades, research into mediumship concentrated on creating a methodology that could not be accused of cheating, fishing or guessing, and that could be made quantifiable, such as that of Julie Beischel. However, much of the early mediumship that involved series of sittings by the same persons provided a personal context that can be more revealing than the factual data that is classifiable as hits or misses. It sometimes offers a continuous flow that is not "... entirely easy to reconcile with the hypothesis of telepathy from the sitters ... There is the joint construction by the medium and her sitters of an appropriate context into which the information fits ..." (Gauld, 2022, p. 139). Such an example is provided by the story of "the mother of Doris" quoted by Gauld. This involves a young woman, Doris Fischer (a pseudonym), who developed multiple personalities after a violent attack by her father when she was three years old. Fortunately, as a teenager, she came into the care of Walter Franklin Prince, who specialised in such conditions. Prince's accounts tell of sittings at which Doris's mother (who had died suddenly when Doris was 15) ostensibly controlled the medium's writing. There is a build-up of detail upon detail of special pet names, of the games that the mother played with the little girl, the quirky and amusing punishments that the mother invented to try to stop Doris from being a danger to herself, and of many other ways in which "Mrs. Fischer emerges from these records as an excellent mother and a charming, humorous person". However, the truly puzzling aspects of these sittings is the extent to which that which "came through" was not just information about Mrs. Fischer, nor about Mrs. Fischer as seen through the eyes of Doris; "it was information about Doris as seen through the eyes of Mrs. Fischer and about their relationship as Mrs. Fischer viewed it and about the worries Doris occasioned her". If this was some dream level of the medium's subconscious mind, obviously also involved in the sittings, "it would certainly require fast footwork and a remarkable level of dramatic skill on the part of that dreaming consciousness." (Gauld, 2022, pp. 225-6). This is not spectacular evidence, it is cumulative and needs close reading, but many older cases with all their details can be very persuasive in making a case for survival.

Clairvoyant virtuosi and mediums learn through experience and practice, but there is one thoroughly described case where it is not practice but preparedness that seems to make the experience possible. David Kennedy describes this experience in a book called *A Venture in Immortality* (Kennedy, 1973). It is a story of an English couple who had the most incredible yet believable experience of communicating with each other, over a number of months, after one of them died. It is obviously not scientific evidence, yet it has a ring of truth and a logic to it that makes sense in the context of what we know about spontaneous cases and the best of mediumship. The middle-class couple, Ann and David Kennedy, met and married in the 1940s. It was a perfect union and total devotion from the start, marred only by Ann's progressive and incurable heart disease.

They became interested in psychical research after David had a puzzlingly accurate and precognitive sitting with a medium. After studying the literature (largely that published by the SPR) and experiencing many sittings with mediums, they became convinced that the human psyche survived the death of the body. David, an engineer by profession, became a minister of the Church of Scotland (where the attitude to mediumship is quite open-minded), and knowing that Ann's condition would not improve they, in a sense, prepared for the inevitable.

After Ann's death, David is naturally grief-stricken, but that does not cloud his judgment. He keeps a detailed diary on which the book is based, and is very much aware that "... proof and evidence are two different things. Proof is the condition when no possible alternative hypothesis can be put forward. It is doubtful if such a condition can be conceived while the human mind remains fertile and imaginative. Evidence on the other hand is the accumulative build-up of facts pointing in a certain direction." (Kennedy, 1973, p. 85). This is what his book sets out to achieve and, it seems as far as possible, succeeds. One important aspect is Kennedy's access to some remarkable mediums, the most remarkable of whom was Albert Best[45].

The book is "one fantastic assembly of coincidences" indicative of Ann's continued presence in and concern for David's life. For example, Best phones David while the latter is frantically looking for a clean clerical collar for a funeral he is about to take, and tells him in which drawer he will find clean collars and how many, and how many dirty ones are in the box for cleaning. This is the kind of exceedingly trivial detail that only a wife would know, unless one is determined to attribute Best's phone call to the latter's clairvoyance. (pp. 105-6)

There are also items of "first class evidence", involving incidents or facts not known to the sitter or the medium. On one occasion Best phones David with a message from Ann that he will shortly learn about some ballet shoes. Ann's sister phones David twenty minutes later, saying she just "took a notion" to call him, and David asks her

---

[45] Albert Best (1917-1996) was a medium and a healer, whose mediumship was described as "of superstar quality" by the late Archie Roy (1924-2012), psychic investigator and professor of astronomy at the University of Glasgow. (Cattenach, 1999/2016, p. 7).

about the shoes. This turns out to have been a private joke between Ann and her sister, based on Ann's attempts to fit into ballet shoes that were far too small for her (pp. 49, 84). Throughout the book there seems to be input from someone who knows what kind of evidence of continued existence is acceptable to researchers; it is a story where what matters is not exactly practice, but preparation for how to handle the attempt of contact and create the right conditions: on the one hand the discarnate Ann keeps coming up with items of information demonstrating her continued presence; on the other, David seeks opportunities for validating those items, with the help of a network of mediums. He is aware of his bias, and describes his book as "tendentious" (p. 156), but his comments reflect a degree of detachment: "this entity, Ann, has memories which are unknown to me" (p. 116); "... if Ann is a creation of my imagination, she appears to be a very curious one. She claims to have a kind of volition of her own ... capable of warning me of a danger in my car, unknown to any human agent" (p. 145). Significantly, Ann does not offer descriptions of the afterlife, and about six months after the first contact she makes it known that she needs to move on and will not be around so often. If one accepts the account as true, and bears mind that these two people had a very close relationship for over 25 years, studied and accepted the evidence for survival, and agreed that whoever died first would attempt to produce the best possible evidence, it would be difficult to design a more convincing experiment than the events described. Clearly though, this is an area where we can only speculate.

Instead of a conclusion

So what do all these in some ways disparate phenomena tell us? From Jackowski, we have a message from Sylvia who intervenes to identify herself as a victim; a promise of no more beatings from a dead husband; a body that wants to be found, or helpful hints about locations that come in words or images (reminiscent of Feda's "sometimes I sees and sometimes I hears"). Mediumship in general provides similar examples of identification and interventions, as well as evidence of personalities with their own point of view, such as the mother of Doris, who, at the time of the sittings, had been dead for some years, yet who "comes through" as if it was a conversation with someone present who is reminiscing. We have the collaborative efforts of the Kennedys, with the crucial input of outstanding mediums, attempting to testify to the continued existence of the discarnate.

And then we have Joe McMoneagle and his outstanding clairvoyance, and his very articulate account of his NDE and its meaning. His experience leads him to believe that he is a small fragment of his totality (McMoneagle, 2013), not confined to the physical; that psychic functioning is an innate human talent, and that inanimate objects with their history also have the potential to play a part in the universal connectedness. In his view of psi, "... the phenomena imply interaction, and that means having properties in common. If discarnate entities are producing actual effects in physical life, by influencing the thoughts and actions of the living, and influencing the behaviour of inanimate objects, then shuffling off the mortal coil cannot be quite the total separation of the mental and the physical that has often been assumed. The mind, the discarnate part, whatever we choose to call it, must have a way of interacting with the physical world. And that discarnate part must also be able to be aware, to reason, to will, and to feel" (McMoneagle, 2012).

That is where the evidence of clairvoyance seems to point. There are important areas of psi where new evidence and new ideas are being examined and developed that relate to the question of survival of bodily death and clearly involve some kind of clairvoyance. Mediumship and near-death experiences have been mentioned in passing, and reincarnation research has not been touched on here. There can be no meaningful discussion of the purpose of psi and the question of survival without this wider context, but that is for other books by other authors. The purpose here has been to add to the evidence for clairvoyance, in a limited cultural context, in the spirit of a true "parapsychological naturalist".

However, the variety of experiences recounted here resonates well with the overview of our current state of knowledge offered by Gregory Shushan in his recent book on near-death experiences in different cultures:

> It is ... conceivable that different postmortem fates await different people, whether determined by culture, belief, or some unknown factor ... There are grounds to believe in the veridicality of NDEs, reincarnation, and perhaps mediumship, and therefore there are reasonable grounds to believe in an afterlife. (Shushan, 2022, p.178).

This surely is a fertile ground for naturalists to bring in observations from different cultures and disciplines, not just parapsychology. There is so much to be learnt about different roles and kinds of consciousness and the ways it integrates with the physical world and whatever might lie beyond. Asking "what is psi for?" at this stage seems too limiting, too focused on the here and now, when the evidence points to its being part of something larger, something we only get glimpses of. So, this does not seem to be the moment for conclusions, but for more exploration as consciousness/intention/information begins to take centre stage in how we view the world.

REFERENCES AND BIBLIOGRAPHY

~

Alvarado, C. S. (2015). 'Out-of-Body Experience (OBE)'. *Psi Encyclopedia*. London: The Society for Psychical Research. https://psi-encyclopedia.spr.ac.uk/articles/out-body-experience-obe. Retrieved 4 February 2021.

Anderson, P.W. (1972). More is different. *Science 177, 4047*, 393-6.

Baker, I.S., Montague, J. & Booth, A. (2017). A controlled study of psychometry using psychic and non-psychic claimants with actual and false readings using a mixed-methods approach. *Journal of the Society for Psychical Research 81, 108-122.*

Barrington, M. R., (2019). *Talking about psychical research. Thoughts on life, death and the nature of reality.* White Crow Books.

Barrington, M. R., Stevenson , I., Weaver, Z. (2005). *A world in a grain of sand: The clairvoyance of Stefan Ossowiecki.* McFarland & Co, Inc.

Beischel, J. (2013). *Among mediums: A scientist's quest for answers.* The Windbridge Institute LLC.

Beishel, J. (2014). *From the mouths of mediums.* The Windbridge Institute LLC.

Beischel, J. (2017). Research in Mental Mediumship, in: Kean, L.: *Surviving death: A journalist investigates evidence for an afterlife.* Three Rivers Press, pp. 170-180.

Beloff, J. (1993) *Parapsychology: A concise history.* The Athlone Press.

Bem, D. J. (2011). Feeling the future: Experimental evidence for anomalous retroactive influences on cognition and affect. *Journal of Personality and Social Psychology, 100*(3), 407–425. https://doi.org/10.1037/a0021524

Boot, A. (1994). *Psychic murder hunters: Real-life stories of paranormal detection.* Headline Book Publishing.

Braude, S. (1994). Does awareness require a location? A response to Woodhouse. *New Ideas in Psychology, vol. 12 No. 1 pp17-21.* Pergamon Elsevier Science.

Braude, S. (2003). *Immortal Remains.* Rowman & Littlefields.

Braude, S. E. (2019). *A parapsychological naturalist. Book review of JOTT: When things disappear ... and come back or relocate—And why it really happens by Mary Rose Barrington.* EdgeScience, 38, 11–12.

Braude, S.E. (2020). *Dangerous pursuits: Mediumship, mind and music.* Anomalist Books.

Broughton, R. (2015). 'Experimental Parapsychology'. *Psi Encyclopedia.* London: The Society for Psychical Research. https://psi-encyclopedia.spr.ac.uk/articles/experimental-parapsychology. Retrieved 26 January 2021.

Cardeña, E. (2018). The experimental evidence for parapsychological phenomena: A review. *American Psychologist* 73 (5), 663-677. https://doi.org/10.1037/amp0000236

Carington, W. (1941). Experiments on the paranormal cognition of drawings. *Proceedings of the Society for Psychical Research 46,* 277-344.

Carpenter, J.C. (2012). *First Sight: ESP and Parapsychology in Everyday Life.* Rowman & Littlefield.

Cattenach, R. (1999/2016). *"Best" of both worlds. A tribute to a great medium.* Saturday Night Press Publications.

Chalmers, D.J. (1996). *The Conscious Mind.* Oxford University Press.

Charman, R. (2021). Empirical evidence of psi healing in mice confirms parapsychology, or psiology, as a legitimate scientific discipline. *Journal of the Society for Psychical Research 85.2,* 91-103.

Cobb, M. (2020). *The idea of the brain: A history.* Profile Books Ltd.

Crabtree, A. (Ed.) (1988). *Animal Magnetism, Early Hypnotism, and Psychical Research, 1766–1925: An Annotated Bibliography.* White Plains, NY: Kraus International.

Dainton, B. (2014). *Self: Philosophy in transit.* Penguin Books.

Davies, P. (2019). *The demon in the machine.* Penguin Books.

Dehaene, S. (2020) *How we learn: The new science of education and the brain.* Penguin Books.

Dingwall, E. (1924). An experiment with the Polish medium Stephan Ossowiecki. *Journal of the Society for Psychical Research, XXI,* 259-63.

Duggan, M. (2020). 'Rex G Stanford'. *Psi Encyclopedia*. London: The Society for Psychical Research. https://psi-encyclopedia.spr.ac.uk/articles/rex-g-stanford. Retrieved 30 January 2021.

Eisenbud, J. (1986). The Denver chair test: Comments from Jule Eisenbud. *Journal of the Society for Psychical Research 53,* 321-324.

Engber, D. (2017). *Daryl Bem Proved ESP Is Real Which means science is broken.* https://slate.com/health-and-science/2017/06/daryl-bem-proved-esp-is-real-showed-science-is-broken.htm

Gauld, A. (1971). A series of 'drop-in' communicators. *Proceedings of the Society for Psychical Research, 55,* pp. 273-340.

Gauld, A. (1995) *A history of hypnotism.* Cambridge University Press.

Gauld, A. (2022). *The heyday of mental mediumship.* White Crow Books.

Gregory, A. (1982). London experiments with Matthew Manning. *Proceedings of the Society for Psychical Research, 56* (212), 283–366.

Grosso, M. (2017). *The final choice: Death or transcendence?* White Crow Books.

Gruber, E.R.(1999). *Psychic Wars: Parapsychology in espionage – and beyond.* Blandford.

Gruza, E. Goc, M. Moszczyński, J. (2008). *Kryminalistyka – czyli rzecz o metodach śledczych [Criminology: on investigative methods],* pdf.

Gurney, E., Myers, F.H., Podmore, F. (1886). *Phantasms of the living.* Trubner & Co.

Hagan, J. C., ed. (2017). *The science of Near-Death Experiences.* University of Missouri Press.

Heywood, R. (1964). *The infinite hive.* Pan Books Ltd.

Heywood, R. (1971). Tribute to Eileen Garrett. *Journal of the Society for Psychical Research 46,* 56-7.

Hoebens, P.T. (1986). Comparisons of reports of the 'Denver' chair test: A critical examination of the methods of W.H.C. Tenhaeff. *Journal of the Society for Psychical Research 53, 311-320.*

Holden, J.M., Greyson, B., James, D. (2009). *The handbook of Near-Death Experiences.* Praeger Publishers.

Honorton, C.(1993). A moving experience. *Journal of the American Society for Psychical Research 87,* 329-340.

Janoszka, K. (2014). *Parapsychologia w pracy śledczej na przykładzie współpracy polskiej policji z jasnowidzem Krzysztofem Jackowskim [Parapsychology in investigative work on the example of the collaboration between the police and the clairvoyant Krzysztof Jackowski].* Unpublished MA Thesis, University of Warsaw.

Janoszka, K. (2018). *Krzysztof Jackowski: Jasnowidz na policyjnym etacie [Krzysztof Jackowski: a clairvoyant with a police job]*. Wydawnictwo Sine Qua Non.

Jones, N (with Davenport, S). (1982). *Ghost of a chance. The life story of a psychic detective.* Pan Books.

Katra, J. (2017). Apparent Communications from an Eager Spirit. *Journal of Scientific Exploration, 31, 2, pp. 293–295.*

Katz, D.L., Grgić, I., Tressoldi, P., Fendley, T.W. (2021). Associative remote viewing projects: assessing rater reliability and factors affecting successful predictions. *Journal of the Society for Psychical Research, 85, 2, 65–90.*

Kauffman-Peil, K. (2015). Emotional sentience and the nature of phenomenal experience. *Progress in Biophysics and Molecular Biology* xxx (2015) 1-18 http://dx.doi.org/10.1016/j.pbiomolbio.2015.08.003

Keen, M. & Playfair, G.L. (2004). A possibly unique case of psychic detection. *Journal of the Society for Psychical Research, 68,* 1-17.

Kelly, E.F. (2018). *Paranormal phenomena, the Siddhis, and an emerging path towards reconciliation of science and spirituality.* In: Presti, D. ed. *Mind beyond brain: Buddhism, science and the paranormal.*pp. 91-120. Columbia University Press.

Kelly, E.F., Kelly E.W., Crabtree A., Gauld, A., Grosso, M., Greyson, B. (2009). *Irreducible mind: towards a psychology for the 21st century.* Rowman & Littlefield.

Kennedy, D. (1973). *A venture in immortality.* Colin Smythe.

Klimuszko, A.C. (Rev). (1989). *Moje Widzenie Świata [My View of the World].* Novum.

Koch, C. (2017). *Consciousness: Confessions of a romantic reductionist.* The MIT Press.

Koch, C. (2019). *The feeling of life itself.* The MIT Press.

Koch, C. (2021). *How Did Consciousness Evolve? An Illustrated Guide.* https://thereader.mitpress.mit.edu/how-did-consciousness-evolve-an-illustrated-guide/

Kocsis, R.N., Irwin, H.J., Hayes, A.F. & Dunn, R. (2000). Expertise in psychological profiling. *Journal of interpersonal violence 15,*311-331.

Koestler, A. (1972). *The roots of coincidence.* Picador Books.

Krakauer, D. Bertschinger, N. Olbrich, E., Flack, J. C., Ay, N. (2020). The information theory of individuality. *Theory in Biosciences 139,* 209–223 https://doi.org/10.1007/s12064-020-00313-7

Lebiedziński, P. (1928) Study of mediumship of Mme Maria Przybylska, an auditive medium. Paper given by the author at the Third International Congress of Psychical Research in Paris on 28 September 1927. *Proceedings of the Institute Metapsychique International, Sept-Oct 1927, Paris 1928,* 124-133.

LeShan, L. (2009). *A new science of the paranormal.* Quest Books.

Luke, D. (2017). *Otherworlds: Psychedelics and exceptional human experience.* Muswell Hill Press.

Lyons, A & Truzzi, M. (1991). *The blue sense: Psychic detectives and crime.* Mysterious Press.

Manning, M. (1978) *The Strangers.* W.H. Allen.

May, E.C. (2014). Invited article Star Gate: the U.S. government's psychic spying program. *Journal of Parapsychology 78*(1), 5–18.

May. E.C. & Marwaha, S.B. (2018). *The Star Gate Archives. Reports of the United States government sponsored psi program. 1972-1995.* McFarland Inc.

Mayer, E. (2008). *Extraordinary knowing. Science, skepticism and the inexplicable power of the human mind.* Bantam Dell Publishing.

McGilchrist, I. (2012/2019). *The master and his emissary: The divided brain and the making of the western world.* Yale University Press.

McGilchrist, I. (2021). *The matter with things.* Perspectiva.

McMoneagle, J. (2000). *Remote Viewing Secrets: A Handbook.* Hampton Roads Publishing.

McMoneagle, J. (2006). *Memoirs of a Psychic Spy.* Hampton Roads Publishing.

McMoneagle, J. (2012). *Interview with Joe McMoneagle.* Skeptiko 3 April 2012.

McMoneagle, J. (1993/1997/2013). *Mind Trek: Exploring Consciousness, Time, and Space Through Remote Viewing.* Crossroad Press (2013 Digital Edition).

Mertz, H. (2020). *The Selection Effect: How consciousness shapes reality.* Penn Wolcott Press.

Mikołejko, A. (2019). *Spirytyzm czy mediumizm? O polskich zmaganiach ze zjawiskami przeczącymi nauce [Spiritism or mediumship? On Polish struggles with phenomena that challenge science].* In: *Polskie tradycje ezoteryczne 1890-1939.* Rzeczycka, M., Trzcińska, I., Mikołejko, A. (eds). Wydawnictwo Uniwersytetu Gdańskiego vol. 2, 38-117.

Morus, I.R. (2005). *When physics became king.* University of Chicago Press.

Myers, F.W. (1903). *Human personality and its survival of bodily death.* Longmans, Green & Co.

O'Keeffe, C. & Alison, L. (2000). Rhetoric in 'psychic detection'. *Journal of the Society for Psychical Research 64*, 26-38.

Osty, E. (1923). *Supernormal faculties in man*. Transl. Stanley de Brath, Methuen & Co.

Palikari, F. (2020). *Angelos Tanagras: Long-distance telepathy experiments*. pdf academia edu.

Price, H.H. (1943). A note concerning the nature of paranormal awareness, *Journal of the Society for Psychical Research 33*, 12-13.

Radin, D. (2018). *Real magic*. Harmony Books.

Randles, J. & Hough, P. (2001). *Psychic detectives: The mysterious use of paranormal phenomena in solving true crimes*. Silverdale Books.

Renier, N. (2008). *A mind for murder. The real-life files of psychic investigator*. Hampton Roads.

Roberts, E. (1969). *Fifty years a medium*. pdf

Robertson, T. (2013). *Things you can do when you're dead*. White Crow Books.

Robinson, C. (with Boot, A.) (1997). *Dream detective. The remarkable true story of how one man's premonitions turned from dream to nightmare*. Warner Books.

Robinson, C. (2006) Psi experiments and how to make sure they fail. *The Paranormal Review 39*, 12-16.

Roe, C.A., Cooper, C.E., Hickinbotham, L., Hodrien, A., Kirkwood, L., Martin, H. (2020). Performance at a precognitive viewing task, with and without ganzfeld stimulation: Three experiments. *Journal of Parapsychology 84,(1)*, pp. 38-65.

Roll, W.G. (2003). Poltergeists, electromagnetism and consciousness. *Journal of Scientific Exploration 17*, 1, pp. 75-86.

Rousseau, D. (2016). *Minds, souls and nature: A systems-philosophical analysis of the mind-body relationship in the light of Near-Death Experiences*. Unpublished PhD thesis.

Rovelli, C. (2018). *The order of time*. Penguin Books.

Rzewuski, S. (1929). Wyniki zbiorowych doświadczeń telepatycznych między Atenami i Warszawą [Results of group telepathic experiments between Athens and Warsaw]. *Zagadnienia Metapsychiczne 23-24*, 36-51.

Schouten S.A. (1981). Analysing spontaneous cases: A replication based on the Sannwald Collection. *European Journal of Parapsychology 4*, 9-48.

Schouten S.A. (1983). A different approach for analysing spontaneous cases: With particular reference to the study of L.E. Rhine's case collection; *Journal of Parapsycholog 47*, 323-40.

Schouten, S.A. (2021). *Psychics and police investigations.* In: *Advances in Parapsychology 10*, eds. Krippner S., Rock, A.J., Friedman, L., Zingrone, N. McFarland.

Schwartz, S.A. (2014). *Through time and space. The evidence for Remote Viewing.* Broderick, D. & Groetzel, B. eds. McFarland.

Semczuk, P. (2014). *Magiczne dwudziestolecie [Magical twenty years].* PWN.

Sheets-Johnstone, M. (1998). Consciousness: A natural history. *Journal of Consciousness Studies* 5 (3), 260–94.

Sheldrake, R. (1998). The sense of being stared at: Experiments in schools. *Journal of the Society for Psychical Research 62*, 311-323.

Sheldrake, R. (2000). Telepathic telephone calls: Two surveys. *Journal of the Society for Psychical Research 64*, 224-232.

Sheldrake, R. (2002). Apparent telepathy between babies and nursing mothers: A survey. *Journal of the Society for Psychical Research 66*, 181-185.

Sheldrake, R. (2005). The sense of being stared at. *Journal of Consciousness Studies*, 12, 4–126.

Sheldrake, R. (2011) *Dogs that know when their owners are coming home.* Arrow.

Sheldrake, R. & Smart, P. (2003). Experimental tests for telephone telepathy. *Journal of the Society for Psychical Research 67*, 184-199.

Shushan, G. (2022). *The next world: Extraordinary experiences of the afterlife.* White Crow Books.

Sinclair, U. (1930/2019). *Mental Radio.* republished by David de Angelis.

Smith, P.H. (2009). *Is physicalism "really" true?* Ph. Dissertation, University of Texas, Austin. (pdf)

Smith, P.H. (2015). *The Essential Guide to Remote Viewing.* Intentional Press. (pdf)

Smolin, L. (2019). *Einstein's unfinished revolution. The search for what lies beyond the quantum.* Penguin Books.

Szczesiak, E. (2000). *Jasnowidz z Człuchowa. Moje tajemnice [Clairvoyant from Człuchów. My secrets].* Polskapresse.

Szmurło, P. (1929). O próbach telepatii między Atenami i Warszawą [On experiments in telepathy between Athens and Warsaw]. *Zagadnienia Metapsychiczne 23-24, December,* 21-35.

Świątkowska, K. & Jackowski, K. (2012). *Zmarli mówią. Autobiografia jasnowidza Krzysztofa Jackowskiego [The dead speak. Autobiography of the clairvoyant Krzysztof Jackowski].* 2 vols. Polskapresse.

Targ, R. (2012). *The reality of ESP.* Quest Books.

Targ, R. & Puthoff, H.E. (1977/2005). *Mind Reach.* Hampton Roads Publishing Co.

Taylor, S. (2018). *Spiritual science.* Watkins.

Tononi, G. & Koch, C. (2015). Consciousness: here, there and everywhere? *Philosophical Transactions R. Soc.* B 370, 1-18.370.

Toynbee, A. Smart N, Heywood R. (1968). *Man's concern with death.* Hodder & Stoughton.

Treffert, D.A. (2010*). Islands of genius; The bountiful mind of the autistic, acquired and sudden savant.* Jessica Kingsley Publishers.

Treherne, A. (2020). *Arthur and me.* Arthur Conan Doyle Centre.

Tyrrell, G.N.M. (1935). Normal and supernormal perception, *Journal of the Society for Psychical Research 29,* 3-19.

van Luijtelaar, M. and Kramer, W. (2020). 'Croiset Archive'. *Psi Encyclopedia.* London: The Society for Psychical Research. <https://psi-encyclopedia.spr. ac.uk/articles/croiset-archive>. Retrieved 11 May 2022.

Vernon, D. (2021). *Dark cognition. Evidence for psi and its implications for consciousness.* Routledge.

Weaver, Z. (2015). *Other realities: The enigma of Franek Kluski.* White Crow Books.

Weaver, Z. (2021). 'Stefan Ossowiecki'. *Psi Encyclopedia.* London: The Society for Psychical Research. https://psi-encyclopedia.spr.ac.uk/articles/stefan-ossowiecki. Retrieved 29 June 2022.

Weber, N. Skeptiko (2008). *Interview with Nancy Weber.* audio: http://content. blubrry.com/skeptiko/skeptiko-2008-11-10-55986.mp3

Wehrstein, KM (2018). 'Kenneth Batcheldor'. *Psi Encyclopedia.* London: The Society for Psychical Research. https://psi-encyclopedia.spr.ac.uk/articles/ kenneth-batcheldor. Retrieved 6 November 2021.

Wehrstein, KM (2019). 'Psychic Detection'. *Psi Encyclopedia.* London: The Society for Psychical Research. https://psi-encyclopedia.spr.ac.uk/articles/ psychic-detection. Retrieved 20 May 2022.

White, R. E. (1964). A comparison of old and new methods of response to targets in ESP experiments. *Journal of the American Society for Psychical Research, 58, 1,* 21-56.

Williams, B.J. (2016). Towards Normalizing the Paranormal: On the Seeming Incompatibility of Science and Psychic Phenomena. *Psychical Research Foundation, 1-27* pdf.

Wiseman, R., West, D. & Stemman, R. (1996): An experimental test of psychic detection. *Journal of the Society for Psychical Research 64*, 34-45.

Zagadnienia Metapsychiczne, Journal of the Polish Society for Psychical Research, Jan/Feb/Mar 1924, p.15.

Zmenak, E. (1972). An Odd Experience Involving a Prediction. *New Horizons, 1, 1*, 61-2.

Zorab, G. (1956). A case of clairvoyance *Journal of the Society for Psychical Research 38*, 244-248.

INDEX

~

www.ingramcontent.com/pod-product-compliance
Lightning Source LLC
Chambersburg PA
CBHW020157090426
42734CB00008B/856